MORE THAN PETTICOATS

Remarkable Michigan Women

MORE THAN PETTICOATS

Remarkable Michigan Women

Julia Pferdehirt

TWODOT®

GUILFORD, CONNECTICUT
HELENA, MONTANA
AN IMPRINT OF THE GLOBE PEQUOT PRESS

A · T W O D O T® · B O O K

Copyright © 2007 Morris Book Publishing, LLC

Text design by Nancy Freeborn
Map by M. A. Dubé © Morris Book Publishing, LLC

Front cover photo: Walking along the beach, Presque Isle, Michigan. Library of Congress, LC-D4-4765.
Back cover photo: Teenagers dressed as suffragists for Halloween, ca. 1912. Courtesy Michigan Women's Historical Center Hall of Fame.

Library of Congress Cataloging-in-Publication Data
Pferdehirt, Julia, 1952-
    More than petticoats. Remarkable Michigan women/Julia Pferdehirt. —1st ed.
        p. cm.—(More than petticoats series)
    Includes bibliographical references.
    ISBN: 978-0-7627-4331-5
    1. Women—Michigan—Biography. 2. Women—Michigan—History.
    3. Michigan—Biography. I. Title. II. Title: Remarkable Michigan women.
    CT3262.M5P48 2007
    920.72—dc22
                                                                        2006029788

Manufactured in the United States of America
First Edition/First Printing

To my own Remarkable Women: Beth, Becky, and Ruth.
You have dared to walk into your dreams. I'm so proud of you.
I love you most in the world! —Mom
Isaiah 44:2-5

CONTENTS

MICHIGAN

ACKNOWLEDGMENTS

Special thanks to Pam and Kent Lorenz and Bill Frostic of Gwen Frostic Studios and Fred Roesti of Peaceways for your kind assistance and enthusiasm for this project. And, to the staff of the Michigan Women's Historical Society, thanks for generosity in time and resources. You are a Michigan treasure.

INTRODUCTION

What an impossible task to choose just twelve from among the thousands and thousands of women in Michigan's history who should be called "remarkable." These twelve include an Ojibwe-French businesswoman who made her fortune in the fur trade, suffrage and antislavery leaders, pioneers and social activists, a barrier-breaking pilot, two artists, and a Slovakian labor unionist. Two women in this volume risked their lives during the Civil War—one as a nurse and the other as a soldier. Each of these women changed her world and the lives of others, both men and women. Each has a unique story of risk, courage, and vision.

Within these pages you will discover Rosa Parks's work for racial justice and equality during the five decades after her famous 1955 bus ride in Birmingham, Alabama. Nancy Harkness Love flies across history's horizon as the first woman pilot to serve in the U.S. military. You'll find Rebecca Shelley, at more than eighty years of age, standing at the gates of the White House, pleading her case for peace during the long years of the Vietnam War.

While Love was flying and Shelley was holding protest signs, Gwen Frostic was pushing the boundaries of creativity and the business world's glass ceiling to make her own way as an artist, entrepreneur, and businesswoman. Marguerite de Angeli, an artist from another small Michigan town, did some boundary pushing of her own as she struggled to keep her dream of writing and illustrating children's books alive while raising a large, active family.

In the 1860s Julia Wheelock Freeman transformed grief at the death of her soldier–brother into a work of healing and compassion as a nurse and relief agent for Michigan troops during the Civil War. At this same time, Sarah Emma Edmonds risked her life for the Union cause as "Frank Thompson," an enlisted man serving in the 2nd Michigan Infantry.

The importance of suffrage and antislavery convictions is underscored by the number of women in Michigan history for whom these issues were a driving force. Laura Smith Haviland, a Quaker widow, risked life, reputation, and livelihood for the cause of racial equality. Anna Howard Shaw defied family, social custom, and religious dogma to pursue her calling as a pastor and outspoken advocate of women's rights. Sojourner Truth used her own story of enslavement and struggle as a weapon against slavery and for human and women's rights.

In her own place and time, Ana Clemenc took an equally risk-laden stand for justice. In Michigan's upper peninsula copper belt, this young woman stood up to thugs, mine owners, and armed militiamen during a miners' strike that shook the entire nation. In the same region, fifty years earlier, Magdelaine LaFramboise navigated power plays and racism in the Indian and European communities and outmaneuvered wealthy white traders to make a success of her murdered husband's fur business.

These women's lives reflect just a few colors in the spectrum of light and beauty found in the history of women in Michigan. Their stories are unique, yet their strengths and qualities of character are found in the lives of women everywhere during every era of history.

MAGDELAINE LaFRAMBOISE

1780-1846

A Bridge between Cultures

IN THE EARLY YEARS OF THE NINETEENTH CENTURY, fur was international currency in the "western" wilds of the new United States. This "frontier," of course, barely reached the Mississippi River. In Michigan and other Great Lakes states, French and French-Canadian voyageurs had been involved in the fur trade business for nearly two hundred years.

French trappers, voyageurs, and traders settled in the Midwest, particularly in fur-rich forest areas near the Great Lakes and nearby rivers. While some spent a few years in America, seeking adventure and wild times before returning to traditional life in France, many men married native women and made the Midwest their home. The community and people that emerged from this blending of cultures were called "Métis," from the French word meaning "mixed."

In 1780 a daughter was born to Jean Baptiste Marcot, a French fur trader well known in the Great Lakes region, and Misigan "Marie" Neskech, daughter of Chief Kewinaquot of the Ottawa tribe. The child, baptized in her father's Catholic religion as Magdelaine, would become a community leader, successful businesswoman, and dedicated supporter of Catholic ministry and missions.

MAGDELAINE LaFRAMBOISE

Magdelaine Marcot spent her early years with her widowed mother. After Jean Baptiste's death, Marie returned to the safety of the Ottawa lands along the Grand River near present-day Grand Haven, Michigan. Magdelaine was raised among her mother's people in traditional ways. However, she was bilingual and her life shows strong influence from her father's Catholic religious heritage.

It is probable that Marie and her extended family received income from fur trapping and trading. Evidence for this comes from church records documenting Magdelaine's baptism, at about age six, at the Catholic mission church on Mackinac Island.

Mackinac was a traditional site for the fur traders' rendezvous, an annual gathering at which voyageurs and local trappers sold their furs. For Ottawa Indians to make the long trek from their Grand River lands in southern Michigan to Mackinac Island strongly suggests they were transporting furs for sale. Perhaps, during one such trading trip, Marie sought out the island's Catholic priest to baptize her daughter.

At about age fourteen, Magdelaine married Joseph LaFramboise, a French-Canadian fur trader. Although this marriage was, at first, *a la façon du pays* (literally, in the manner or custom of the country), the couple formalized their union about ten years later before a priest named Fr. Jean Dilhet on Mackinac Island. They also brought their children to St. Anne's Church on Mackinac Island for baptism—Josette, born in 1799 when Magdelaine was only fifteen years old, and Joseph, born in 1806.

It was common for Métis couples to first formalize their relationship within the Indian community and then to ask a priest, when available, to witness their vows and marry them within the legal structure of the Catholic Church. This practice reflected the melding of cultures in the Métis community.

Today Joseph would be described as a middleman in the fur trade. He bought furs from Ottawa trappers and sold them at Mackinac Island. At first furs were purchased from middlemen or directly from trappers by investor-backed groups from Europe. One of the best known of these groups was the Hudson Bay Company, which was established in the 1600s. In 1822 American entrepreneur John Jacob Astor undercut the European competition by establishing trade between U.S. business interests and local fur traders.

Joseph and Magdelaine followed the fur trade in a semi-nomadic life. They wintered in Ada, Michigan, near present-day Grand Haven. There they built a trading post, the first mercantile establishment in Ada. They traded with area Indians, purchasing animal pelts with such trade goods as blankets, axes, iron or brass cooking pots, knives, household goods, and guns. All winter they accumulated furs.

In spring they loaded the furs onto bateaux—flat-bottomed, low boats. They hired local Ottawa men as boatmen and made the long journey up the coast of Lake Michigan to Mackinac Island. They relied on income from the furs to purchase more trade goods and other necessities during the rest of the year.

In the fall of 1806, with an infant in tow, Magdelaine and Joseph returned from Mackinac Island. About a day's journey from Grand Haven, they stopped for the night on a beach. At some point, a native man asked Joseph for alcohol. Joseph refused, and the man returned that evening and shot him.

In an instant Magdelaine was left widowed with two young children. She ordered the boatmen to load Joseph's body into a bateau and she took him to Grand Haven to be buried. Then she did what was necessary to support herself and her children.

Before Joseph's sudden and shocking death, Magdelaine had been an active participant in their fur-trading business. She used her language skills to negotiate with area Indian trappers by speaking Ottawa, Ojibwe or Chippewa, French, and English. But, with her husband dead, she could either return to her Ottawa family or take over the fur-trading business herself. She chose to continue the business.

Women were rare, although not unknown, in the fur trade. Some Métis women had achieved some success in this largely male-controlled business. For the next six years, until the War of 1812 disturbed relationships between French, English, Indian, and U.S. communities, Madame LaFramboise ran her business much as she and her husband had done. Yearly trips to Mackinac Island cemented relationships with fellow Métis traders and the Catholic mission church. History records that she was a shrewd businesswoman. Under her leadership the business grew.

Therese Marcot Schindler, Magdelaine's older sister, was one of the Métis women living on Mackinac Island. Therese had married a Protestant fur trader from the island in 1804. After poor health forced her husband to retire, the couple started a school for boys. Therese followed in her sister's footsteps and continued to make a living in the fur trade. The two women remained close.

During the first decade of the nineteenth century, John Jacob Astor, an American businessman, entered and began to change the fur trade. His American Fur Company gained a foothold in the Great Lakes Area. However, the War of 1812 hurt Astor and other trading companies. Some trading posts were lost to the British.

One by one, Astor forced his competitors out of business. He pressured Canadian traders to sell their enterprises in U.S. territory. While many of her counterparts became bankrupt, unable to compete with Astor's growing operation, Magdelaine remained independent and successful.

Then, in 1817, the American Congress passed a law expelling all foreign fur traders from U.S. lands. This placed almost the entire American fur trade directly under John Jacob Astor's control. Suddenly Magdelaine had to deal with a monopoly run by an Oregon-based business known for cutthroat tactics and the crushing of all opposition. Flexibility was the key.

In the years following Magdelaine sometimes worked independently and sometimes worked directly for Astor's American Fur

Company. In 1818 her name appears on a list of employees, listing her as "employed at Grand River." In 1922 records indicate she was again trading independently with local trappers.

Independent trading was risky. Traders were required to obtain a federal license to trade each year. Indian and Métis traders were sometimes the victims of racism on the part of government officials. Large companies sometimes bribed officials to deny licenses to competitors.

One of Astor's methods of extending his control of the market was to refuse to buy furs from independent middlemen. Because Magdelaine had many contacts and relationships within the Indian communities in the region, she had ready and abundant sources for furs. She knew the best trappers and the most successful families or tribal clans. However, when she bought those furs, she always risked the possibility that Astor would refuse to purchase them or that his growing business had swallowed up all other potential buyers.

Still, Magdelaine was successful. She used her language skills and relationships within the native communities to build sound trading relationships. Perhaps local trappers preferred trading with the daughter of an Ottawa chief to strangers from the American Fur Company.

During these years Magdelaine straddled the French and Indian worlds. She sent her daughter, Josette, to Montreal to be educated, and Josette became more European than Indian. In 1815, at about age sixteen, Josette met and fell in love with Capt. Benjamin K. Pierce during a winter stay at Mackinac Island. Pierce was stationed at Fort Mackinac during the unstable years after the War of 1812.

Josette and Benjamin Pierce married in a small ceremony, perhaps conducted by a military officer, at Mackinac Island on April 2, 1816. Evidently, Magdelaine was away, probably still collecting furs in Grand Haven in preparation for the spring selling.

When Magdelaine returned to the island, she held a second wedding for the couple at a friend's large home. Captain Pierce's fellow officers, their families, and two leading Métis families from the island community were welcomed by Madame LaFramboise herself and her sister, Therese, both formally dressed in traditional Ottawa clothing.

In 1819 Madame LaFramboise accompanied her son, Joseph, to school in Montreal. This journey, which took weeks, was made by canoe. Magdelaine was nearly forty years old. Joseph remained in Montreal with his father's relative, a nephew named Alexis LaFramboise. Magdelaine paid for Joseph's education herself.

Records seem to indicate that during the next decade, Madame LaFramboise sold the trading post she and Joseph had established to a Grand Haven fur trader. For some time she worked as an agent for John Jacob Astor's American Fur Company. Then Astor purchased the LaFramboise company outright. Magdelaine LaFramboise became a very wealthy woman.

The LaFramboise trading operation was a lucrative one. When Astor bought the business, history records her "retiring" to her beloved Mackinac Island, where she invested herself and her considerable fortune in the people and matters she valued most.

Madame LaFramboise believed education was crucial to success. At significant cost, she ensured that Josette and Joseph received the best education Montreal could offer at that time. After Josette and her infant son died in 1821, Benjamin Pierce left their daughter, Josette Harriet, with Magdelaine. Then, it appears, he abandoned the family. Magdelaine took responsibility for raising and educating Josette Harriet.

Magdelaine's support of education extended beyond educating her own family. In 1823, Rev. William Ferry, a Presbyterian missionary, requested her help in establishing a school on the island. Madame LaFramboise first offered part of her own home to be used by the school, the Reverend Ferry, and twelve boarding students.

With a school operating in her home, Magdelaine took the opportunity to learn to read and write. Documents show that in

1821 she could speak four languages but was unable to write even her name in any of the four. By 1830 she had learned to read and write both French and English. She used those skills to teach the Roman Catholic catechism to children.

Madame LaFramboise became increasingly important in the Mackinac Island community. When the Reverend Mr. Ferry found a permanent location for his school, Magdelaine opened her home to other visitors and guests. She often acted as hostess to island visitors while wearing traditional Ottawa dress.

Indian Agent Henry Schoolcraft, for whom the Michigan community of Schoolcraft is named, was a guest in her home and wrote about her in his journal.

John and Juliette Kinzie visited Madame LaFramboise during their journey from Detroit to the emerging Lake Michigan harbor city of Chicago. Juliette wrote *Wau-Bon,* one of the early eyewitness histories of the settlement of the "northwest." In it she called Mackinac Island "that gem of the Lake." About Madame LaFramboise she wrote, "It was her custom to receive a class of young pupils daily at her house, that she might give them lessons. . . . She was a woman of a vast deal of energy and enterprise—of a tall and commanding figure and most dignified deportment."

In 1831 French aristocrat and writer Alexis de Tocqueville visited Mackinac Island during his extensive travels in America. De Tocqueville was delighted to meet an articulate, multilingual native woman. Because the two could converse in French, he interviewed Madame LaFramboise at length about her Ottawa ancestry and culture.

Margaret Fuller, a writer, critic, and international reporter for the *New York Tribune,* visited the island in 1843. Fuller wrote about Magdelaine, describing her as "wearing the dress of her country. She spoke French fluently . . . They were all the time coming to pay her homage or get her aid and advice, for she is, I am told, a shrewd woman of business." Mackinac Island so impressed Fuller that she wrote about it in her memoir *Summer on the Lakes.*

Fuller's perception of Magdelaine's role and position within the island community was accurate. Madame LaFramboise was a bridge between the Métis and both the French- and English-speaking communities. While it is possible that some visitors were curious or even amused by the sight of an English-speaking, wealthy woman in traditional Ottawa dress, history records the deep respect by which she was held by those who knew her.

Magdelaine knew times were changing and that her people, the French and Métis, would have to change with them. The culture of French, Indian, and Métis fur traders would soon be swallowed up by American culture, business, and government. She knew education in English and French would be critical to the survival of the next generation. To that end she educated both her children and granddaughter in Montreal. Then she invested considerable money in schooling for Métis and Indian children on the island.

Within fifty years Métis culture would largely disappear. By 1850 fur had fallen out of fashion in Europe. The market collapsed and John Jacob Astor transformed fur storage buildings on the island to transfer sites for fish.

Even in relatively undeveloped regions such as northern Michigan, the once comfortable blending of French and Indian cultures was forever altered by the influx of Euro-American immigrants, decades of broken treaties and stolen lands, and the U.S. government's forcible removal of Indian peoples.

Magdelaine was also a bridge between the Catholic and Protestant communities. A lifelong, devout Catholic, she opened her home to a Presbyterian mission school and contributed funds to the school when the Reverend Ferry found it a permanent location.

Until 1830 Mackinac Island was without a permanent Catholic priest. Magdelaine faithfully prayed the Angelus, a Catholic prayer liturgy, at six o'clock in the morning, at noon, and at six o'clock in the evening. The bells of St. Anne's Church rang each day to mark these hours.

In the 1920s a new church building was needed, and Magdelaine donated land adjacent to her house. Church records show that, in thanks, the church assigned her pew number one and exempted her from the annual pew rental fees. Magdelaine's request was that she be buried under the altar of the new church house.

In 1830 Fr. Samuel Mazzuchelli, an Italian missionary priest from the Dominican order, was commissioned as the "missionary priest of the whole Northwestern Territory." He was assigned to St. Ann's Church on Mackinac Island.

Upon arriving on the island, Father Mazzuchelli made a temporary home with Madame LaFramboise and assumed responsibility as pastor of St. Ann's Church. Magdelaine gave personal, administrative, and financial assistance to Father Mazzuchelli to establish a school for Catholic children. The school opened, and within a short time twenty-six children were enrolled. One of the teachers, Martha Tanner, had been a student at Reverend Ferry's Presbyterian school. Tanner represented the second generation of island children for whom Madame LaFramboise had helped to provide an education.

Madame LaFramboise took her position as a community leader quite seriously. Much of her wealth was used for her Mackinac Island community. When Schoolcraft visited the island in 1837, he noted that she had provided food and financial assistance for "a poor, decrepit Indian woman" who had been abandoned by her family. After her death, the reading of her will revealed a bequest of $50 for the "most poor of the Island."

Magdelaine raised her granddaughter, Josette Harriet, and remained on the island with her sister, Therese, until her death in 1846 at the age of sixty-six. As she had requested, Madame LaFramboise was buried under the altar of St. Ann's. Many years later, when a basement was added to the church building, her remains were relocated to the churchyard.

Magdelaine's will reflected her interests and loyalties. Her home was left to Josette Harriet Pierce and the remainder of her estate to her son, Joseph, a successful businessman living in Montreal. Small bequests included one hundred dollars given to a niece who was a teacher of Métis children on the island. Historians have noted that, although Madame LaFramboise was wealthy and enjoyed sterling tableware and some imported furniture, in general, her possessions were few and relatively simple.

Magdelaine LaFramboise was a founding mother of the Mackinac Island community. During her lifetime she saw her beloved island grow from a rendezvous site and fishing community to a destination for wealthy adventurers and lovers of natural beauty. She witnessed the establishment of a permanent ministry at St. Ann's Church and the growth, peak, and decline of the great fur trade in North America.

Today, Magdelaine's house still stands on Mackinac Island as the Harbour View Inn. And visitors and residents alike still worship at St. Anne's Church, located next door on land donated by Madame LaFramboise nearly 180 years ago.

SOJOURNER TRUTH

1797–1883

A Sign to the Nation

ABOUT 1797, JUST TWENTY YEARS AFTER THE SIGNING of the Declaration of Independence, Isabella VanWagenen (sometimes rendered VanWagener) was born in the city of Hurley, Ulster County, New York. The freedom for which Americans had so recently fought wasn't extended to this newborn child, or to her parents or siblings. They were slaves, the property of Col. Johannes Hardenbergh, a Revolutionary War veteran.

Isabella was the youngest of thirteen children born to James and Betsy. Eleven sons and daughters had been sold or died. Only Isabella and her brother Peter remained.

Isabella's father, James, was also known as Bomefree—a Dutch word meaning "tree." His first and second wives had been sold before he married Betsy, a gentle woman called Mau-Mau Bett.

James and Betsy had some comforts. They lived in a small cottage and grew tobacco, corn, and flax on the colonel's land. Of course, James and Betsy didn't own the land or house. But they had some privacy and a home for their little family.

SOJOURNER TRUTH

When Isabella was about three years old, Colonel Hardenbergh died. Isabella, Peter, James, and Betsy became the property of his son, Charles. Years later, Isabella remembered Bomefree and Mau-Mau Bett saying they were fortunate because, unlike the rest of the Hardenbergh family, Master Charles was kind.

However, Isabella didn't remember kindness. She did remember moving to Master Charles's new stone house and hotel. Upstairs, the Hardenbergh family and hotel guests lived in comfort. Isabella's family and the other slaves did not. All day they cooked, cleaned, and did the work of running the hotel and household. Each night they slept in the cellar—men, women, and children together in one cold, damp room. Loose boards covered the dirt floor. Chill and wet seeped through thin blankets. Sleep was interrupted with the coughing of sick people. When Bomefree and Mau-Mau Bett suffered from rheumatism and fever sores, Isabella blamed the damp cellar for causing their pain.

James and Betsy had suffered so much loss. Again and again, Betsy told Isabella and Peter how their older brother Michael and sister Nancy had been taken away. The story pressed itself into Isabella's memory. Fifty years later, as a free woman using her chosen name of Sojourner Truth, Isabella still recalled every detail.

Five-year-old Michael had woken early. Snow had fallen, and the small boy rushed outside to see a horse-drawn sleigh carrying two men in front of Colonel Hardenbergh's house. A man put Michael in the sleigh. Then the man entered the house. Michael was terrified when the man returned carrying little Nancy. The men locked Nancy in the sleigh box. Michael screamed for Mau-Mau Bett. He leaped from the sleigh, fled into the house, and hid beneath a bed.

Like thousands of enslaved parents before and after them, James and Betsy were helpless to intervene as the slave traders took their children. They never saw Nancy or Michael again. Mau-Mau Bett turned to God in her pain and loss. Betsy's faith shaped Isabella's character and became a foundation for her life.

When Isabella was nine years old, Charles Hardenbergh died, leaving thousands of dollars of debt. His property, including Isabella, Peter, and Betsy, was to be sold to pay those debts. But what about Bomefree? His health had failed. A lifetime of too much work and too little rest had left him too crippled for physical labor. As far as the Hardenbergh family and the slave traders were concerned, Bomefree was worthless. Who would pay to support a slave who couldn't work?

The Hardenberghs chose to do what many slave owners did with slaves too old or sick to work. They emancipated Bomefree and Betsy. After a lifetime of service, the old couple would be left to support themselves. Perhaps the Hardenberghs considered themselves generous. After all, Bomefree and Betsy would be "free."

But Isabella and Peter went to the auction block. For about $100 the little girl was sold to Mr. John Neely. Life had always been hard for Isabella, but, in that moment, as she wrote years later in her autobiography, *The Narrative of Sojourner Truth,* "the war had begun."

Isabella was taken from her parents and brother. At nine years old, this Dutch-speaking child became the only slave in the Neely's home, where only English was spoken. When Isabella didn't understand orders, she was beaten. Without shoes or warm clothes for winter, she suffered frostbite. Once John Neely beat the child with a bundle of sticks until her flesh was torn and bleeding. The scars remained for life.

Years later when Sojourner Truth described brutal beatings in slavery, she spoke from personal experience. In her autobiography she wrote, "When I hear them tell of whipping women on the bare flesh . . . my very hair rises on my head. Oh! My God! What a way is this of treating human beings?"

This abuse lasted two years. At about age twelve, Isabella was sold to a fisherman and tavern owner named Scriver. She became an all-purpose servant, carrying fish, picking corn, fetching herbs to make beer, and hauling liquor from town. The workload was brutal, but at least no one beat her.

Just one and one half years later, in 1810, Isabella again was thrown into the unknown. The Scrivers sold her to John Dumont for about $175. She was determined to avoid beatings by working hard. However, Isabella would learn that hard work wouldn't guarantee kindness or even safety.

Isabella did household labor for Sally Dumont and worked in the fields for Mr. Dumont. Mrs. Dumont found fault with everything Isabella did. The white hired girls took every opportunity to elevate themselves and keep the "colored girl" in her place. Once a hired girl named Kate threw ashes into a pot of potatoes Isabella had washed and peeled, and Isabella was beaten for carelessness.

Only John Dumont took Isabella's side. In her autobiography, Sojourner wrote that he called her Bell and boasted to his friends, "that wench is better to me than a man—for she will do a good family's washing in the night, and be ready in the morning to go into the field where she will do as much . . . as my best hands."

Isabella, then a young teenager, behaved like many abused children. Historian Nell Irvin Painter noted in her scholarly study of Sojourner Truth's life that Isabella was hungry for affection and approval. Isabella worked long hours. Sometimes she slept leaning against a wall, snatching a little rest before returning to work. She worried constantly that her work wouldn't be acceptable. If Mr. Dumont praised her, the hired help and fellow slaves taunted and mocked. She admired and trusted Mr. Dumont. During her years as Dumont's slave, she even accepted his belief that slavery was good and honorable.

At age sixteen or seventeen, Isabella met and eventually loved Robert Catlin. Some historians think Robert may have been the father of Isabella's oldest daughter, Diana. But for enslaved people, even love, marriage, and parenthood were controlled by slave owners. Robert was owned by Dumont's neighbor, Mr. Catlin. Catlin knew children from a marriage between Isabella and Robert would legally be Dumont's property, so he refused to allow the relationship.

When Mr. Catlin discovered the couple together, he and his sons beat Robert brutally. This beating, it seems, damaged more than skin and bone. Robert's spirit was broken. He returned to the Catlin farm, married a fellow slave at Catlin's demand, and died within a few years.

Before Isabella reached her twentieth year, she married Thomas, an older man also enslaved by the Dumonts. Like Catlin, John Dumont knew enslaved couples could produce a "harvest" of children for the fields or the auction house. Either way, he would profit. Isabella and Thomas did not disappoint; between 1815 and 1826 Isabella gave birth to five children while working in both the field and house. Mr. Dumont's $175 "investment" paid richly, year after year.

For decades abolitionists had demanded an end to slavery in New York state, and in 1817 an emancipation law was passed. Slave owners protested that they'd be bankrupt if their slaves were freed. So a gradual emancipation was planned. Adults born before 1799 (which would include Isabella and Thomas) would be freed in ten years, on July 4, 1827. Any slave born in 1800 or later would remain in slavery until age twenty-five for women and age twenty-seven for men.

Mr. Dumont promised "Bell" that if she worked faithfully, he'd free her and Thomas—though not their children—in 1826, a full year before the law required. Along with "free papers," he promised them a cottage and a small piece of land. Years later Sojourner Truth said she dreamed of gathering her children around a fire in their cozy cottage. Some historians believe she planned to remain in the promised cottage with her children until the entire family was freed.

So for nine years, Isabella and Thomas worked. Three or four more children were born. Sometime in 1825 Isabella's hand was badly injured, limiting her ability to work for a time. In July of 1826 Isabella asked Mr. Dumont for the promised freedom. Dumont refused, claiming Isabella's injured hand had kept her from doing enough work. She and Thomas, Dumont demanded, would remain his slaves for another year.

Isabella was trapped. The hope she'd lived on for nine years was gone. The "free papers," cottage, and land were just lies. And, even when Isabella and Thomas became free, their children would still be Dumont's slaves for decades.

In that moment the obedient Isabella who worked so hard to please Mr. Dumont began to change. She finished the spinning work and then took her baby, Sophie, and fled. This was her first step toward becoming a new person—a free woman who would some-day call herself Sojourner Truth.

Isabella hid with the Van Wagenen family, who paid John Dumont twenty-five dollars to release her from a final year of slav-ery. During this time, Isabella had a religious experience. Often, during her many years as a speaker and preacher, she described the moment recorded in her autobiography when she realized "in the twinkling of an eye, that God was all over . . . that there was no place where He was not."

Meanwhile, John Dumont sold Isabella's son Peter. The boy was only five years old. To prevent slave owners from escaping the finan-cial loss of emancipation by selling their human property elsewhere, New York law forbade selling slaves out of state. However, Peter was sold to an Alabama plantation owner. Isabella actually filed and won a lawsuit against a white man to recover her son.

The lawsuit took every dollar she had. In 1829, perhaps seek-ing better-paying work, Isabella moved to New York City. She rarely spoke of the painful decision to leave Ulster County. Her marriage to Thomas had ended. Her daughters Diana, Elizabeth, and Sophie remained the property of the Dumont family.

As Isabella worked in New York City, she desperately missed her children. Perhaps that longing for family left her vulnerable to a religious movement called the "Kingdom of God." She left New York City and gave everything she had—savings, furniture, and labor—to the group and its charismatic leader.

After a few years scandal destroyed the "Kingdom of God." Falsely accused of poisoning a fellow member, Isabella returned to New York City, still searching for spiritual meaning. In June of 1843 Isabella told a friend that God was calling her to preach. Her name would no longer be Isabella, but Sojourner Truth, because she would be a traveler. She was to tell anyone who would listen about God's truth. She wrote in her autobiography, "The Spirit calls me there, and I must go."

So, having arrived in New York as Isabella Van Wagenen, she left as Sojourner Truth. She headed east and spoke in churches and at temperance meetings. Listeners were amazed to hear this simple, black woman speak so eloquently about spiritual matters usually left to men with seminary training.

According to Truth's autobiography, one Connecticut man sent her to friends in Hartford with a note saying, "Please receive her and she will tell you some new things. . . . She has got the lever of truth, that God helps her to pry where few can. She cannot read or write, but the law is in her heart. . . . H. L. B."

People were drawn to the novelty of a black woman preaching. But if they expected amusing song and dance, they were disappointed. Sojourner Truth spoke with power and passion about God, goodness, and faith. Sojourner traveled through Massachusetts, Connecticut, New York, Ohio, Pennsylvania, Indiana, Wisconsin, Illinois, Missouri, and Kansas. At first, she preached; then, in 1844 in Northampton, Massachusetts, she spoke for the first time against slavery. For the next twenty years, she spoke at antislavery gatherings.

Abolitionist leader William Lloyd Garrison encouraged Sojourner to speak personally about slavery. In 1850 Garrison helped her publish *Narrative of Sojourner Truth*. Priced at twenty-five cents, the autobiography provided income for Sojourner, who had seen a ready market for her story and had borrowed money to publish it.

Between 1850 and 1860 the issue of slavery was ripping the nation apart. Northern states passed emancipation laws, and Sojourner Truth and similar speakers drew audiences of the curious and the passionate. During her speaking tours in the Midwest, Sojourner met Lucretia Mott and Laura Haviland, two Quaker abolitionists and women's rights leaders.

Some of Sojourner Truth's speeches are well known. At the 1851 Ohio Women's Rights Convention, she sparked a fire by saying, "If a woman has a pint and a man a quart, why can't she have her little pint full? You need not be afraid to give us our rights . . . for we can't take more than our pint'll hold. The poor men seem to be all in confusion and don't know what to do."

Sojourner spoke for her race and gender. A now-famous narrative records her baring her arm, saying, "Aren't I a woman?" and declaring women weren't "weaker vessels." Hadn't she worked as hard as any man?

In 1852 Sojourner and Frederick Douglass attended an antislavery meeting in Salem, Ohio. In despair, Douglass said the only choice was for black people to rise up in violence. Sojourner replied as one friend to another, saying, "Frederick, is God gone?"

Douglass included this story in his own autobiography. He wrote, "We were all for a moment brought to a stand-still, just as . . . if someone had thrown a brick through the window."

Mott and Haviland invited Sojourner to speak in Haviland's Battle Creek, Michigan, home. Battle Creek was involved in the antislavery and Underground Railroad networks and home to a community of free and self-freed black people. There Sojourner met some peace-loving, unprejudiced Quakers who called themselves the Progressive Friends. The "Friends" ran an integrated school and founded Harmonia, a racially mixed community. In 1857 Sojourner sold her home in Massachusetts and moved to Michigan.

Battle Creek became a sanctuary. Her daughters Elizabeth and Diana and some grandchildren joined her. Perhaps the old dream of gathering her family in a fire-lit cottage was finally becoming reality. From this sanctuary Sojourner traveled to Washington, D.C., to meet Abraham Lincoln.

By 1863 the Civil War was under way. Sojourner's grandson, James Caldwell, enlisted in the Massachusetts 54th, the first black Union regiment. Nineteen young black men from Battle Creek joined the Michigan First Colored Infantry Regiment. Sojourner Truth was with these men in heart, if not in body. In November 1863 the First Colored Infantry Regiment was training at Camp Ward in Detroit. Sojourner went door to door collecting food for the soldiers' Thanksgiving Day dinner.

In February Sojourner brought more food and clothing from the people of Battle Creek. She spoke to the soldiers and even sang her own words to the *Battle Hymn of the Republic*. The words, recorded in her autobiography, were, "Look there above the center where the flag is waving bright; We are going out of slavery, we are bound for freedom's light; We mean to show Jeff Davis how the Africans can fight, As we go marching on."

Battle Creek was Sojourner's "base." She traveled to Washington, D.C., working with the Freedmen's Bureau. She campaigned for government funds to educate and employ former slaves. She recruited abolitionist friends to pressure Congress to resettle freed blacks on "government" land in the West. Sojourner Truth dreamed that before she died the West would become a peaceful home for her people.

During these years, Frances Titus, a friend from Battle Creek, became Sojourner's helper and coworker. By the mid-1870s, when she was approaching eighty years of age, Sojourner suffered what might have been a stroke. The illness left her partially paralyzed and with serious ulcers on her legs. In 1876 a rumor spread that she had died. But she wasn't ready to give up yet.

In 1875 Frances Titus wrote *Book of Life,* a biography written in collaboration with Sojourner, to complete the *Narrative of Sojourner Truth* published twenty-five years earlier. Sales from Titus's book provided some income for Sojourner when she was unable to travel.

In 1879 Sojourner went to Kansas to make one more effort to convince the government to help former slaves become self-supporting landowners. Michigan friends, including Laura Haviland and Elizabeth Comstock, joined her. But the government ignored them, and in 1880 Sojourner returned to Battle Creek. She continued her work for racial equality and women's suffrage.

Sojourner was more than eighty years old, and her daughters living with her in Battle Creek were themselves grandmothers. The leg ulcers and infection that had plagued Sojourner in 1876 returned. Friends visited and prayed, hoping she would rally as she had in the past. But, that wasn't to be.

Early on November 26, 1883, Sojourner Truth died. More than a thousand people attended her funeral. She was buried in Oak Hill Cemetery. As news spread that Sojourner Truth had finally gone to meet the God she loved, she was mourned by thousands across the nation who had been her friends and coworkers in the long fight for freedom, racial equality, and women's rights.

LAURA SMITH HAVILAND

1808–1898

A Woman's Life Work

IN 1864 A TINY, GRAY-CLAD QUAKER WOMAN ARRIVED AT the Union army encampment at Fort Pillow, Tennessee. Laura Smith Haviland brought with her funds, volunteers, and "missionary barrels" filled with clothing. Haviland, a known abolitionist and women's rights activist, had traveled from her hometown of Raisin, Michigan, to help thousands of self-freed slaves seeking sanctuary with Union troops.

People fleeing from slavery, called contraband by military officials, often showed up terrified, half-starved, and ragged wherever federal troops were found in numbers. These refugees were willing to work, but their immediate needs were enormous. At Fort Pillow, news of the desperate need for clothing reached Laura during breakfast shortly after her arrival. Five little boys who were almost naked had arrived.

Haviland wrote in her autobiography, *A Woman's Life Work: Labors and Experiences of Laura S. Haviland:*

> The adjutant told me . . . he had given one little fellow a pair of
> his own pants. I told him to bring them to the commissary tent.

. . . Soon we were . . . measuring, fitting, and handing out, when up stepped the little fellow of eight summers with the tall man's pants, rolled over and over at the bottom. One suspender tied around him and the other placed over his shoulder to hold them on. His eyes sparkled. . . . On the other side stood a little girl who exclaimed, in surprise, "Oh Milla, my dress has a pocket and see what I found." She drew out a rag doll two inches long. Then, a dozen other little girls instituted a search and found similar treasures, which I recognized as coming from certain little girls in Hudson, Michigan. All were on tip-toe with excitement.

Laura Smith Haviland's life story was one of great loss and struggle, punctuated with scenes of compassion and courage and people like the children of Fort Pillow. The violence and horror she witnessed during her lifetime was at odds with her gentle demeanor and deep faith.

Haviland's undaunted efforts to help fleeing slaves meant her life was threatened and her safety in question on many occasions. Slave catchers and bounty hunters offered rewards for her death. Public officials in Michigan pressured her to abandon her vision to educate black children. Neighbors called her a "rabid abolitionist."

Born in 1808 to Canadian Quaker parents, Laura Smith was a serious, spiritual child. As a teenager, she struggled with questions of faith. While many young people spent their time reading "penny dreadful" novels and adventure tales, Laura read and reread the history of the slave trade written by British abolitionist leader John Woolman. Laura was marked for life by that brutal history. She would spend her money, time, and compassion for the people about whom Woolman wrote.

Faith and a deeply personal, experiential relationship with God also marked Laura Haviland. All her life she had very "un-Quakerlike" spiritual experiences, including visions and prophetic dreams that accurately foretold future events. However, for many years she told

LAURA SMITH HAVILAND

no one about these dreams and visions. She recorded them secretly and decades later shared them in her autobiography.

In 1823 Laura Smith married Charles Haviland. The couple settled in what was then Michigan territory. For them, settling meant more than just finding work and housing; they searched for the nearest Quaker meeting to meet their spiritual needs. However, Charles and Laura immediately found themselves caught in a tug-of-war within the Quaker movement.

Although Quakers had long been opposed to slavery, during the 1820s the Society of Friends, as the Quakers called themselves, was torn by disagreement about how that opposition should be carried out. Since helping people escape from slavery was illegal, some Quakers saw abolitionism as inconsistent with biblical requirements to be honest and law-abiding. Others thought true faith required them to wait until God himself intervened, as when the ancient Israelites were saved from slavery in Egypt. Still others held that aiding fugitive slaves was a matter of following the biblical command to "obey God and not man."

Laura and Charles resigned from the Society of Friends. In a letter explaining their departure, they wrote, "We claim higher law." They called slavery "wicked enactments of men." As a young bride, Laura Smith Haviland set her mind and convictions to the freedom of slaves. Her often-expressed moral standard was: WHATEVER PRIVILEGE . . . I CLAIM FOR MYSELF, I CLAIM FOR EVERY OTHER HUMAN BEING IN THE UNIVERSE, OF WHATEVER NATION OR COLOR.

The year 1837 found Charles and Laura in Raisin, Michigan, a rural community in Lenawee County. Located near territorial roads linking the Ohio border and Detroit, Raisin was a center of abolitionist action.

The Havilands established a school for "poor-house" children. Raisin Institute taught basic literacy and religion. Boys learned farming, and girls learned sewing and homemaking skills. The institute followed the ethical and educational model of Oberlin College, the first school of its kind in the United States to admit women and blacks.

In an era when illegitimate and minority children and girls from poor families were frequently abandoned to illiteracy, Laura and Charles admitted any child of good character, regardless of race, gender, or patrimony.

Neighbors were horrified. Government officials tolerated the education of poor white children because the skills they gained kept them from being dependent on public charity. However, the Raisin Institute policy to admit and educate any black child in need raised the hackles of racist Northerners. One official even hinted that funds to support the school might be "found" *if* the Havilands stopped admitting black students.

By 1845 Charles and Laura Haviland were parents to seven children. In early March Laura experienced one of the dreams that would both haunt and shape her entire life. She dreamed that an airborne angel astride a stallion approached the Haviland's house just as the sun rose. Laura's father and mother, her sister Phoebe, and her husband were in the yard. In Charles's arms, as the dream unfolded, was their youngest daughter. The angel said, "Let the dead bury their dead, but follow thou me."

Within weeks an epidemic, believed to be either a virulent influenza or rheumatic fever, overwhelmed the region. By the end of April, all the family members—and only those members—who appeared in Laura's dream were dead. Left widowed with six dependent children, Laura nearly succumbed to the illness herself.

The death of Charles Haviland left Laura alone and facing seven hundred dollars owed in pending debt payments. She estimated the potential income from the wheat harvest, and some friends helped with immediate needs. One man to whom the estate owed money told Laura that she could not possibly manage her husband's business affairs. He counseled her to hire a trustworthy man to manage her money and property. Of course Laura had no money to hire anyone.

She wrote in her autobiography, ". . . although these words were not unkindly spoken, yet they were saddening to my already sad heart."

The family's financial survival was made possible by the sale of forty acres of land. Some debts were delayed and others were forgiven by generous friends. All the while, Raisin Institute continued. There were students to be fed and taught. Her own children were still recovering from the loss of their father, grandparents, and baby sister, and as Laura wrote, ". . . fugitive slaves were still making their resting-place with us."

Laura continued the abolitionist work she and Charles had begun. During the intensely difficult summer and harvest season of 1845, Laura hired one "self-freed" man, George Taylor, to help with hay making and harvest. She recorded his story, one of many narratives about slavery, escape, and abolitionist work recorded in Haviland's autobiography.

George had unsuccessfully tried to gain his freedom. He was caught and "placed in irons, until they made deep sores around his ankles. . . . Being so badly crippled, he was thought safe. But, supplying himself with asafetida, which he rubbed over the soles of his shoes to elude the scent of bloodhounds, he followed the north star. . . . His ankles were still unhealed."

Neither widowhood nor financial struggles dimmed Laura Haviland's desire and willingness to help escaping slaves. She had founded the Logan Female Anti-slavery Society of Michigan. Her home and property became a safe house. In fact, this widowed mother of six children was so well known to slave owners that a bounty was placed on her life. "Patrollers" as slave hunters were called, cursed the tiny woman to her face and threatened her in her own home. And for seventeen years Haviland regularly wrote letters of encouragement to Calvin Fairbanks, an Oberlin College graduate imprisoned in Kentucky State Penitentiary for helping people escape from slavery.

In 1850 the federal Fugitive Slave Law was passed. This granted "recovery" rights to every slave owner. The law stated that enslaved people were not human beings with legally defined rights; they were "property," rightfully and legally belonging to their owners. Fugitive slaves, or as Haviland called them, "self-freed" slaves could legally be captured and returned to bondage. An astonishing and controversial element of the law was the provision allowing law enforcement officers to deputize and force any male citizen of legal age to assist in the "return of property." The passage of the Fugitive Slave Law of 1850 caused abolitionists to step up efforts to assist self-freed people in their escape to Canada.

Haviland's involvement in the antislavery and Underground Railroad movements drew her into a world she never would have known as a churchgoing, spiritual wife and mother. She was lied to and threatened by slave hunters. She aided one young woman, barely out of her teens, who had been sold as a "fancy girl." Haviland's help kept this child from a life of forced prostitution and abuse.

John Chester, a Kentucky slave owner, once held a pistol inches from Haviland's face and promised to kill both her and her son Daniel. Only the timely arrival of local abolitionists saved her life.

Haviland's autobiography seems part spiritual reflection and part horror story. She writes of prayer and deep peace about her children's future. She recounts stories of divine providence and guidance. She also tells, in detail, about her face-to-face experience with slavery and slave holders.

During the late 1850s, she befriended a former slave from Arkansas. The man, whom Haviland called "Charles McClain" to disguise his identity, had a sister still in slavery. After consulting with abolitionist leader Levi Coffin, Haviland traveled to Little Rock to see if she might be able to help "Charles's" sister escape.

There Haviland experienced realities of slavery she had previously only heard about. She stayed in the home of a slave owner and witnessed the brutal beating of two children for failing to light the house fires before the mistress awoke. She listened to the whispered stories of a father torn from his family and parents whose children had been sold away from them.

After traveling to Arkansas, Haviland became increasingly vocal and radicalized. She obtained cast-iron devices designed to prevent slaves from moving freely and displayed them, along with leg irons, chains, and heavy metal yokes used to contain and punish, at public meetings and abolitionist forums. To any who would listen, she told stories to which she was an eyewitness.

Of course aiding and supplying people bound for Canada cost money. Although she always lived simply, Haviland asked anyone and everyone for help. She was not too proud to beg for people in need. Once she crossed the state line to raise funds in an Ohio border town. Some businessmen ridiculed her and denied her request. Mr. Lyons, the town banker, boasted that he'd give five dollars for every dollar she raised from an abolitionist.

Haviland approached acquaintances and total strangers. She repeated Mr. Lyons's pledge and, as a result, received more than twenty dollars for the cause. However, when she arrived at Mr. Lyons's office, the man declared that none of the donors was a real abolitionist. He defined a "real abolitionist" as one who stole legal property and perpetuated the lie that slaves were mistreated and beaten and children sold away. Haviland wrote that she could only wish this man would see his wrong thinking before he died and could make no amends.

Financial strain plagued Raisin Institute, so Haviland helped others found a school in Toledo, Ohio, for the purpose of educating free and self-freed blacks. With her daughter Anna, she taught more than one hundred little children in the basement of Zion Church in Cincinnati. Then she spent a year establishing a school in Windsor, Ontario.

In 1861 the Civil War began. The fact that many politicians and regular citizens alike cared little about slavery and were concerned only with keeping the nation united didn't deter Haviland. She closed Raisin Institute and volunteered to care for soldiers as a nurse.

She assisted prisoners of war. "Every soldier," she said, "was some mother's son." Military hospitals filled her with horror. These filthy places killed as many soldiers through disease as bullets took on the battlefield. Haviland became an advocate, writing countless letters and badgering both military and government officials for aid.

Often, the men in charge assumed this middle-aged, motherly woman would be easily dismissed. They were wrong. In one hospital Haviland discovered an army surgeon too drunk to safely operate. She went straight to the commander and refused to budge until the surgeon was removed from duty.

In 1864 Haviland visited Ship Island, a military prison near the Union-conquered and Union-controlled port and city of New Orleans. There she found more than three thousand Union soldiers imprisoned for minor offenses such as drunkenness or being late at roll call. The presiding judge, Judge Attocha, a secret Confederate sympathizer, had sentenced every man to a long prison term.

Haviland had come to bring bibles and "spiritual comfort." She expected to find hardened criminals. Instead she discovered three regiments' worth of loyal soldiers broken down by unjust imprisonment. One man had been sentenced to fifteen years of hard labor for drunkenness. Another gave army rations to a local resident in exchange for coffee and received eight years of labor with a ball and chain.

Haviland was horrified. Judge Attocha outranked the prison administrators, who feared they also would be imprisoned if they defied him. The prisoners managed to get into Haviland's hands a petition pleading with army command to intervene.

Haviland dedicated herself to freeing these soldiers. She returned to New Orleans and began a one-woman campaign. This grandmother talked her way into generals' tents. She attended a Christian Commission meeting for the sole purpose of cornering any and every officer and government official present with pleas for the Ship Island prisoners. In her autobiography Haviland told how she pressured, lectured, and, at one point, spoke to a group of passive officers "as if they were ten year olds."

Within a couple of weeks, Haviland's pleas and the shocking truth about Ship Island had made its way up the army chain of command. Judge Attocha was dismissed, and the prisoners were freed and returned to their regiments.

Although service as a nurse was needed and worthwhile, Haviland's deep commitment to fighting slavery soon led her into different work. She began to gather clothes, funds, and volunteer teachers to meet the needs of the thousands of people fleeing slavery for the presumed safety of the Union army camps. She did whatever she could for those the army called contrabands and whom she called in her autobiography "these stripped and lonely ones."

One of her first trips was recorded in her autobiography. When news came through abolitionists' circles that more than one thousand fugitive slaves were arriving daily at Union encampments in Cairo, Illinois, Haviland begged and cajoled until she'd gathered a substantial store of donated clothing, shoes, blankets, and food. She departed for Chicago with only fifteen dollars in cash and no means of travel to Cairo. On the way she met a government official who gave her documents for free train travel.

Thus began more than a decade when Haviland used her Michigan home as a base for service. Sometimes linking with Baptist Home Mission work, sometimes with government or private efforts to establish schools for freedmen, Haviland poured her life and energy into meeting immediate physical needs for food and clothing and long-reaching needs for education, spiritual encouragement, and hope. After the war's end she was employed by the Freedmen's Aid Commission at a salary of forty dollars per month.

She traveled from city to city recruiting volunteers and setting up "day schools" for children and mothers and "evening schools" for adults. Again Haviland saw needs and responded. After assessing needs and starting schools across Kansas, Haviland attempted to send some orphaned children to Michigan. She even sold the Raisin Institute building and surrounding acreage with plans for it to be turned into an orphanage. The state government refused to allow an orphanage to be established, saying the children would be a burden on the taxpayers.

Haviland represented the Freedman's Committee in Washington, D.C., during the turbulent postwar years when refugees crowded the nation's capital seeking help. Haviland, though approaching age sixty, became a force for justice. When she discovered aid was being denied black refugees, she raised such an outcry that government officials were forced to distribute aid more equitably. Obtaining funds from her own sources, she walked from dwelling to dwelling seeking out people in need.

Throughout this time Haviland was a source of information for others. She spoke to women's groups, abolitionist gatherings, and temperance meetings. She exposed horrific practices, like lynching, Ku Klux Klan activity, and the 1879 rape and murder of a black woman in Mississippi. These stories helped convince the postwar North that black citizens were still in need of support and protection.

In her later years Haviland joined Susan B. Anthony and others working for women's suffrage. Her autobiography, written in 1881, includes detailed records of her work with the Underground Railroad network, her establishment of freedmen's schools, and both her refugee-relief and prison-reform efforts.

Laura Haviland died in 1898, having spent more than sixty years laboring for justice, freedom, education, and the rights of both blacks and women. Today a memorial statue erected in Adrian, Michigan, honors her lifework.

JULIA WHEELOCK FREEMAN

1833-1900

Michigan's Florence Nightingale

HAD THE CIVIL WAR NOT VIOLENTLY interrupted, Julia Susan Wheelock might have passed an anonymous, peaceful life teaching school, attending church, and taking tea with friends. Instead she left job, home, and family to spend nearly the entire Civil War with the Michigan Relief Association, serving in military hospitals. In makeshift, often dirty, ill-equipped, and crowded hospitals, she fought the death and disease that were the natural companions of war.

At age twenty-one Julia Wheelock made Michigan her home after the death of her mother. In 1858 she enrolled at Kalamazoo College, a small, progressive school that was one of a handful of colleges admitting female students. Julia studied Latin and higher math. At her graduation she obtained a teaching position in a tiny school in Ionia, a rural community located in the countryside between Grand Rapids and Lansing.

Three days before the end of the 1862 school year, Julia received a message at school. "Orville is wounded. . . . He has sent for Anna, and she starts for Washington tomorrow." In this abrupt

JULIA WHEELOCK FREEMAN

way, Julia Wheelock learned that her beloved brother, Orville, had been wounded at the Battle of Chantilly.

On September 23, 1861, Wheelock's brother, Orville, had been mustered into Company K of the 8th Michigan Infantry Volunteers. After training and a brief assignment in Detroit, he joined his regiment in Washington, D.C., the following summer. Between July and December of 1862, the 8th Michigan and the Army of the Potomac fought some of the Civil War's bloodiest battles. In the end the 8th Michigan lost nearly seven hundred of its seventeen hundred men.

August 28 to August 30, 1862, the 8th Michigan fought in the Second Battle of Bull Run, a costly Confederate victory. Union troops retreated, and the next day, on September 1, with Confederate troops in pursuit, the 8th Michigan engaged in another terrible battle, the Battle of Chantilly Plantation. Fighting in a downpour, Union forces lost sixteen thousand men and Confederate losses exceeded nine thousand men. Among the wounded was Orville Wheelock. It had been Orville's first battle.

In the chaos after the battle, Orville laid in a muddy field for several days before being taken to the field hospital. There his left leg was amputated. He was finally taken to a military hospital at Alexandria, Virginia. On September 10, the news reached Michigan.

On September 11, Julia Wheelock, her sister Sarah, and her sister-in-law Anna left for Washington. After two days of exhausting travel, they reached the capital. What they found was terrifying. Wounded soldiers were cared for at fourteen different "hospitals"— converted hotels, schools, churches, and former residences of Washington's wealthy citizens.

Soldiers from any one state or even from a single regiment might be located anywhere. Frantic relatives such as Julia and her sister-in-law had no way to find their loved ones but to search from building to building, ward to ward, and even bed to bed. The women were sent from one hospital to the next; in each instance they were told Orville was recovering somewhere else. They trudged across the city. Then, at the Lyceum hospital they were met by a soldier who told them Orville had died the day before news reached Michigan. He had already been buried in the Alexandria soldiers' cemetery.

The only comfort offered the grieving women was to see the mound of dirt at grave 207. A nurse, Clara Jones, had been with Orville as he died of infection. Julia wrote in her memoirs that it was a small but precious comfort to know that, at least, Orville hadn't died alone.

Sarah and Anna returned to Michigan. Julia Wheelock had been so deeply moved by the suffering and need in the hospitals, she decided to stay and help in any way possible. She joined the Michigan Relief Association. This largely volunteer organization had formed in the autumn of 1861 for the purpose of supporting Michigan soldiers.

The situation in which Wheelock and other "visiting agents" of the Michigan Relief Association found themselves was overwhelming. Sick soldiers lay in filthy conditions. In the hospitals themselves such basic needs as cooked food and clean clothing were difficult to obtain at best and often nonexistent.

Wheelock and a fellow Michigan volunteer, nurse Elmina Brainard, soon became friends and coworkers. Some days they would spend ten to twelve hours moving from building to building and bed to bed while caring for wounded men from Michigan.

During these months and, eventually, years, Wheelock kept a personal diary. About the hospitals she wrote, "In my visits to these hospitals I seldom went empty-handed; sometimes taking cooked tomatoes or stewed fruit, at others, chicken broth, pickles, butter, cheese, jelly, tea hot from the stove, and . . . I would frequently buy oranges, lemons, and fresh fruit. . . . I gave out clothing to those most in need."

Wheelock and Brainard visited a "half-way" facility about one and a half miles from the city. There, wounded men, overflow from the hospitals, and those too ill or not ill enough to be hospitalized languished in a place called "Camp Convalescent" by the military and "Camp Misery" by the men. Conditions were appalling.

Wheelock described life in Camp Misery in her memoirs by penning, "Here were ten to fifteen thousand soldiers—not simply the convalescent, but the sick and dying . . . some with not even a blanket . . . the wonder will be, not that they died, but that any recovered."

Wheelock soon discovered red tape at every turn. Her job was to meet physical needs for ailing soldiers. She cooked, distributed clothing and blankets, and often obtained hot, soapy water, rolled up her sleeves, and cleaned filthy quarters. Needed supplies often were held up or detoured by military bureaucracy, and Wheelock and her fellow agents were forced to plead their cases for the need of essential materials before army officers or medical doctors. Although much of the labor and caregiving was done by women agents and nurses, the men in charge held all decision-making authority. In time Wheelock grew weary of seeing men die when adequate care could have been given. She became unwilling to accept the often arbitrary decisions of those in authority.

"Towards the latter part of November I learned from bitter experience the meaning of the phrase, 'red tape,'" she wrote in her diary. One day she visited Camp Misery and found several Michigan soldiers sleeping on bare ground without benefit of fire, food, or medical attention. Wheelock could predict their untimely and unnecessary deaths unless they were transferred to a hospital.

She approached the commanding officer for permission to transfer the soldiers. He deferred to Dr. Jacobs, the surgeon in charge. Dr. Jacobs was gone, and Wheelock found herself shuttled from one person and office to the next. A surgeon, Dr. Robertson, agreed to accept the soldiers as patients if Wheelock could arrange their transfer.

Finally, Wheelock solved the problem by resorting to what she called "a practice I had always greatly abhorred, that of kidnapping.

. . . But, in this business I never had—as many kidnappers must have—any remorse of conscience. . . . I stole with the free will and consent of the stolen."

The next day was Sunday. Early in the morning Wheelock sent for an ambulance and started for the camp. Since no one else seemed willing to take responsibility, she decided to do what needed to be done. Acting as if she were under orders, she transported six men to Dr. Robertson's hospital.

Some years later, Wheelock actually met one of her "kidnapped" men in Portland, Michigan. He thanked her, saying she had saved his life.

Michigan charities, churches, and communities gathered needed resources for wounded soldiers. Often Wheelock and her colleagues were responsible for distributing desperately needed food, clothing, blankets, and even pillows. She also witnessed misuse of goods sent for soldiers.

In her memoir Wheelock observed the harsh realities of medical care in any hospital in the 1860s. Without antibiotics and armed with relatively primitive surgical techniques, physicians and nurses often were left to "wait and hope for the best." Wheelock recorded the devastating numbers lost to fever and infection. Sometimes typhoid, pneumonia, or even smallpox swept through entire hospitals in a tidal wave of death.

Wheelock's memoir is filled with references to faith, prayer, and heaven. In addition to the motivation of her personal faith, belief in heaven and hope in God were often the only recourse for wounded soldiers and those who cared for them.

One of Wheelock's tasks was to sit with dying soldiers. She often wrote letters to loved ones "back home." She was aware of the importance of those words, often the last contact a family or friend would have with a soldier who would be dead by the time the correspondence arrived.

As the front lines of battle changed, so did the location of hospitals. A field hospital always was set up by the army close to encampments. But seriously wounded men or those needing more care than a hit-and-run field operation could provide were sent to quasi-permanent facilities, usually set up in the largest buildings available within a reasonable distance from the front. This meant, of course, that when battle lines shifted suddenly, Wheelock and the medical teams found themselves in the path of advancing enemy troops.

In July 1863 Wheelock was serving at a makeshift hospital in the former "Stoughton House" in Fairfax, Virginia. She recorded in her memoir that a messenger arrived "in great haste from division headquarters to the hospital department with orders to hoist a 'red flag' early the next morning, for it was reported that rebel troops under the command of General Robert E. Lee were advancing in the direction of Fairfax."

Wheelock and the other women went to work making two large, red, fabric flags to be displayed from the roof and windows of the building. Wheelock noted in her diary that, although it wasn't impossible that rebel troops would fire upon the hospital, the real danger was from renegade bands of guerrillas, who were allied with neither side and used the war as a cover for murder and theft.

The women decided to remain with the wounded soldiers and take their chances, although battles flared on every side of their location at Beverly Ford, Rappahannock, and Aldie. After nearly a week of the constant sounds of cannon fire and a steady influx of wounded, Wheelock looked out to see the approaching wagon train of the 12th Army Corps. By day's end the whole Army of the Potomac was camped around Stoughton House.

The great Army of the Potomac remained for a few days and then headed toward the site of a head-on collision between Federal and rebel troops: Gettysburg. The hospital was emptied and would be relocated near the new battlefront. Wheelock was left behind to pack valuable and hard-to-obtain goods, such as bedding, medicine, and food. She was assured that a transport would be sent. She waited and worked alone in the remains of the Stoughton House. She waited so long that she'd actually prepared a "little speech" recorded in her diary to give to Confederate General Moseby, in case rebel troops reached Fairfax before the transport.

A driver finally arrived, and Wheelock brought her supplies, through a steady rain and wheel-clogging mud, to safety in Washington. The next day headlines in the local newspaper announced "Moseby at Fairfax Court House." The accompanying article noted that two Union ladies in Fairfax had been taken captive.

While Union and Confederate troops battled across the Pennsylvania farmland and mountains, Wheelock was assigned to Baltimore, where some wounded soldiers from Gettysburg were being sent. She pleaded to be sent directly to Gettysburg, where the need was greatest, but she accepted her assignment and threw all her energy into doing what she could at the six Baltimore hospitals.

In Baltimore Wheelock noted in her diary an unusual occurrence. Evidently rebel women claiming to be Union sympathizers brought to the hospital bandages and blood-absorbing lint that was sprinkled with cayenne pepper. When placed on wounds, the pepper caused excruciating pain. Men died from the inflammation and infection that resulted. Wheelock was scarcely able to comprehend that such cruel acts could be done by women.

Wheelock's diary describes an ongoing battle with bureaucracy and power-wielding men. Surgeons in charge sometimes barred her and other volunteers from "their" hospitals. Sick men were found without blankets or warm clothing. Discharge papers were often delayed so long that the affected soldier contracted some disease in the hospital and died of it.

Often new arrivals from the front were not only wounded but also hungry. Wheelock wrote in her memoir of preparing chicken soup "enough for 400 men." On many days Mrs. Brainard or another volunteer spent twelve hours cooking while Julia Wheelock delivered the food. The women often hand-fed soldiers too ill to feed themselves. Their purpose, as they saw it, was to meet any need, no matter how basic or difficult.

By 1864 Wheelock was delivering supplies directly from the Michigan Relief Association to Michigan troops. Outside Alexandria, Virginia, she entered a Union encampment searching for the 26th Michigan Regiment. During her search she visited the field hospital, a single one-story log cabin with a rough, axe-hewn wooden floor. "Cots" were pine boughs and a blanket. She delivered supplies that were actually earmarked for Michigan men to every wounded and sick soldier in sight.

Wheelock and the Michigan Relief Association volunteers followed the lines of battle, helping to set up and then move hospitals. Arriving in Washington, D.C., with plans to spend some weeks in Michigan, Wheelock changed her mind when she saw the overwhelming influx of wounded men. Her brother's own 8th Michigan marched through the city, heading toward the Battle of Wilderness. Wheelock watched until the last man departed, thinking of her dead brother.

In spring of 1864 Wheelock was transferred to Fredericksburg. There she met Miss Clara Barton, a nurse whose name would become known in nearly every American household by the war's end. And there she confronted the most horrible conditions to date in her service.

One field hospital was set up in a former grocery store, and wounded men lay like cordwood, filling every bit of floor space. When Wheelock arrived there wasn't any food, and open wounds were untended and sometimes infested with vermin. A single candle lit the room. She simply rolled up her sleeves and began her work.

In Fredericksburg city, trainloads of wounded arrived daily. Wheelock wrote in her memoir that ten thousand wounded soldiers were housed in the city at one time. Every public building and many private residences had been pressed into service. "Fredericksburg," her memoir records, "was one vast hospital." The women of the Michigan Relief Association and other volunteer groups worked nonstop. Sleep was snatched when possible. Filth and blood and dying men were everywhere.

Many volunteers, like Julia Wheelock, had come from educated middle- or upper-class families, and their past lives had been sheltered. No more. The women cleaned and bound open wounds, changed dressings, hauled and delivered goods, cooked, and scrounged for needed supplies. Wheelock saw amputated limbs piled outside surgeons' tents. Once she found a group of wounded men waiting, without any medical care, in a filthy building. She walked two miles in searing heat to insist that a surgeon and nurses be sent. Then she walked home, loaded supplies, and headed back to the men.

In early July 1864, Gen. Ulysses S. Grant visited the relief workers at their station near Appomattox. Wheelock took note of his exhaustion and genuine desire to bring the war to an end.

In August Wheelock returned to Michigan to recover from a bout with typhoid fever and exhaustion and to raise money for relief work. By early winter of 1865, she had spoken to groups and individuals across the southern half of the state. Her diary records $450 in donations, ranging from $2.75 collected at a Dutch church to nearly $300 raised by women at "Oyster suppers" in cities and small towns.

In April Wheelock returned to Washington, D.C.; Lee had surrendered at Appomattox. The war, though not the suffering, was over.

On the day of Lincoln's assassination, Wheelock was in Washington. After so much death and suffering, Lincoln's death was an emotional tipping point for her and for the nation. Wheelock viewed Lincoln lying in state both at the White House and the Capitol. She wrote in her memoir, "It seemed he must only be sleeping, that he would soon awake, but alas! He sleeps the sleep that knows no waking."

Still grieving and not entirely recovered from her earlier illness, Wheelock launched into hospital work again. Wounded and sick men arrived in Washington by the thousands. Michigan's and other relief associations established houses for men from their states. The arrival of peace stood in stark contrast to the death arriving daily on troop trains and in wagons. Wheelock recorded story after story of dying soldiers from Michigan in her diary. "I might continue to enumerate such instances for nearly every ward in our hospitals," she wrote, "but the memory of them is too painful."

Wheelock witnessed the formal "grand review" of the army by its new commander in chief on May 23 and 24, when an estimated one hundred and fifty thousand troops "passed in review" in the nation's capital. Officers rode in full uniform. Troops marched in formation. Crowds placed wreaths around the necks of officers and enlisted men. Her diary makes special mention of Michigan troops and the Army of the Potomac marching under "tattered banners" brought from the battlefield.

Julia Wheelock's service with the Michigan Relief Association ended in July of 1865, and at home she was called "Michigan's Florence Nightingale." She remained in Washington and worked at the Treasury Department for eight years. In 1870 her diary was published as a book titled *The Boys in White: The Experience of a Hospital Agent In and Around Washington.*

Then in 1873 she returned to Michigan and married Porter C. Freeman of Middleville. Two sons, Frank Wheelock and Frederick Orville, were born in 1876 and 1879, respectively. Later the family moved to Springfield, Missouri, where they lived until Julia's death in 1900.

After her "army life," Julia Wheelock never expressed regret at spending three years in such terrible and violent conditions. She wrote in *The Boys in White* of "both joy and sorrow." She reflected on the opportunity to observe "every trait of the human heart . . . not only the evil . . . but also the God-like virtues."

"Best of all," Julia Wheelock concluded, was "the consciousness of doing good; but the sad reflections far outweigh all the pleasant experiences."

SARAH EMMA EDMONDS

1841–1898

Soldier, Nurse, and Spy in the 2nd Michigan Infantry

ON THE SECOND DAY OF THE BATTLE OF BULL RUN, a soldier from the 2nd Michigan Infantry hurried toward the front lines, leading a mule loaded with mail for Berry's Brigade. Knowing that battle was imminent and the letters precious, the soldier took every shortcut he knew. Near Centreville he tried to cross a ditch, and the mule reared. The soldier was thrown to the ground and trampled by the terrified animal. He laid stunned and injured in the ditch until he recovered enough to crawl toward the mule. Dragging his left leg and coughing blood, he clung to the mule and struggled on toward the Union lines.

The infantryman, Frank Thompson, was badly injured. However, he refused to see the doctor when he reached his regiment. He told friends that if the doctor knew his lungs were injured, he'd be sent home.

During Thompson's two years in the 2nd Michigan Infantry, he earned the respect of officers and fellow soldiers. He volunteered to nurse wounded men and served as a spy in Confederate territory. However, Frank Thompson was a soldier with a secret. Frank Thompson was actually Sarah Emma Edmonds.

During her lifetime, Sarah Emma claimed many identities in name and role. As young Sarah Emma Evelyn Edmonson in Dumfrie Parish, New Brunswick, Canada, she helped her frail mother and tried unsuccessfully to please her abusive father. In a post-Civil War memoir entitled *Unsexed, or the Female Soldier,* Sarah Emma described her early life as "sheltered but enslaved" and her father as the "stern master of ceremonies."

When she was sixteen, Sarah Emma's father decided to rid himself of one daughter. He agreed to marry Sarah Emma to a neighbor. She was frantic. As wedding preparations proceeded in the farmhouse kitchen, Sarah Emma ran away. With help from her mother and a distant cousin, she became Emma Edmonds, a salesgirl in a millinery shop.

The milliner's shop was a place of peace until her father discovered her whereabouts. In 1858 Emma Edmonds fled again. This time she changed more than her name.

Years later, details of Emma's disappearance came to light. She'd seen an advertisement for jobs selling bibles and religious books, so Emma cut her hair, spent her savings on men's clothing, and applied for the job. She was hired and began her life as Franklin Thompson.

As a child in New Brunswick, Sarah Emma had once read a "penny dreadful" novel left by a peddler as payment for a meal and night's lodging. The novel, *Fanny Campbell, the Female Pirate Captain!* told the fanciful story of a "noble looking girl" who could row a boat, shoot a gun, and ride horses. To save her unjustly arrested sweetheart, Fanny went to sea disguised as "Seaman Channing."

Some historians and overimaginative writers have theorized that Sarah Emma disliked her gender and routinely dressed as a boy in childhood. Others have suggested she was homosexual. This isn't

SARAH EMMA EDMONDS

consistent with Edmonds's life or words. In a newspaper interview conducted after publication of her memoirs, Sarah Emma described men and marriage as unsafe. She said she'd thought about taking a man's identity after reading *Fanny Campbell*. Sarah Emma used male clothing and identity to gain freedom denied women, but she consistently perceived herself as female. During and after her years masquerading as Frank Thompson, she expressed romantic attraction toward men.

What is apparent is that becoming Franklin Thompson protected Sarah Emma from an unwanted marriage and the restrictions of travel, work, and autonomy placed by society upon nineteenth-century women. As a sincere, young bible seller, Frank Thompson accomplished what Sarah Emma could not. He made money and became a self-supporting, independent adult. And, Frank had adventure!

As Frank, Sarah Emma was a success. She canvassed the countryside, hawking bibles and religious books door to door.

Sarah Emma went to Hartford, Connecticut, in search of more profitable work. As Frank, she crossed the border on foot, and somehow her inventory and money were lost. She sold her last bible and pawned her watch and chain to buy a decent suit and shirt, knowing she'd have to make a respectable appearance to land a job.

In her memoir Sarah recorded that Frank entered a publishing office and inquired whether they "had any use for a boy who had neither money or friends, but was hard to beat on selling books."

Evidently the owners were amused and impressed by Frank's straightforward self-confidence. Mr. Hurlburt invited the "young man" home for supper, introducing him to his family with a chuckle and the words, "He's hard to beat on selling books."

Frank's new employers sent him to Nova Scotia. In ten months, this book-selling wonder made nine hundred dollars—an impressive income in the 1850s. Frank's boss wrote that in thirty years they hadn't employed a better salesman. For Frank this was a time of grand adventure.

Sarah Emma wrote, "I went to Nova Scotia in February and returned in November . . . I lived well, dressed well, and gave away more money to benevolent societies than in all the rest of my life. I came near to marrying a pretty little girl who was bound I should not leave Nova Scotia without her."

A slogan of the time was "go west and grow up with the country." Frank decided to go to Michigan, where he boarded with Charles Pratt in Oakland County and continued to sell books for Mr. Hurlburt. Once Pratt declared Frank handled a pitchfork like a woman. Frank quickly stated he'd never done farmwork in his life. One might say that, since it was Sarah Emma who worked her father's fields, "Frank" was telling the truth.

Within the year Frank moved to Flint and boarded with a Methodist minister who did double duty as captain of the Flint Union Greys. This patriotic group became Company F of the 2nd Michigan Infantry. Although Frank was Canadian, when the Union Greys enlisted, he did too.

The Civil War was in full fury. Sarah Emma wrote in her memoir, "I felt called to go and do what I could for the defense of the right. If I could not fight, I could take the place of someone who could and thus add one more soldier to the ranks."

However, Frank was rejected. He was two inches shy of the minimum height requirement. Company F left for training without him, but Frank persisted. That spring he enlisted as a field nurse. On May 25, in Detroit, Private Franklin Thompson was officially inducted into the United States Army.

About ten weeks later, Frank and the 2nd Michigan Infantry joined green, nearly untrained recruits at the Battle of Bull Run. For many it was their first and last battle. More than five thousand soldiers died on both sides.

In 1865, under her own name, Sarah Emma Edmonds wrote *Unsexed, or the Female Soldier.* Later that title was changed to *Memoirs of a Soldier, Nurse, and Spy.* The memoir presented a somewhat romanticized picture of Frank Thompson's military career based on Frank's journals.

Edmonds's telling of the Union defeat at Bull Run offers no romance. It describes the brutality and horror of battle, death, and defeat.

After Bull Run, the 2nd Michigan Infantry transferred to Washington, D.C., and the Army of the Potomac. General George McClellan, a West Point–educated engineer, was commander. Although McClellan was an incompetent commander, Sarah Emma credited him with bringing discipline to the defeated troops.

With Chaplain and Mrs. Bindell, Frank served the 2nd Michigan as a field nurse. Fighting was fierce, with rebel troops protecting and Union troops trying to capture the Confederate capital of Richmond. Frank saw shattered bodies and witnessed hundreds of deaths. He saw amputated limbs piled beside surgeons' tents.

At Fort Monroe, Frank met contrabands—fugitive slaves seeking asylum with Union troops—perhaps his first face-to-face encounter with black people.

At Yorktown, Frank was amazed by "balloon reconnoissances." Colonel Lowe, a college-professor-turned-army-colonel, used a hot-air balloon to site enemy troops. Frank was fascinated. In her memoir, Sarah Emma recounted one "reconnoisance" when the balloon tore from its moorings. Union troops could only watch in horror as the balloon and its passenger drifted over rebel lines. The slightest descent would have put the man in firing range. At the last minute, it seemed, the wind turned and the balloon drifted north again.

As a field nurse Frank purchased food and supplies. Outside Yorktown he purchased eggs and butter from a secret Confederate sympathizer. First the woman tried to delay Frank, all the while watching at the window. Frank guessed she was expecting someone. Rebel soldiers, perhaps? As Frank rode from the woman's home, she fired a pistol, barely missing him. Frank turned, pulled his "seven-shooter" firearm, and shot the woman through the hand.

Frank determined to turn his assailant in to the Union commander. Tying her one wrist to his saddle, he pulled the woman along for some distance. Eventually his prisoner fainted from exertion and blood loss. Frank washed and bandaged the woman's hand and put her astride his horse, still intending to deliver her to General McClellan.

As they traveled the woman told him that within three weeks she had lost her father, husband, and two brothers in the war. These losses had nearly taken her sanity. She'd taken her grief and anger out on Frank. The woman sobbed and apologized, over and over, for shooting at him. She said she would pay for her crime by nursing wounded soldiers if Private Thompson would only change his plan to turn her in to General McClellan.

In her memoir Sarah Emma wrote that "Alice . . . but we called her Nellie" seemed truly sorry. If she had been a man, no doubt Private Thompson would have killed her. Instead, Frank remembered a bible verse saying, "If thy brother sin against thee, and repent, forgive him."

So, Frank delivered the woman into the care of the camp physician. When her hand was healed, she kept her promise and, in Sarah Emma's words, "became one of the most faithful and efficient nurses in the Army of the Potomac."

A few days later one of Frank's closest friends was killed. Frank was angry; he wanted revenge against the rebels for killing his dear friend. In her memoir Sarah Emma wrote that the pain and grief of that loss helped her better understand "the feelings of poor Nellie when she fired the pistol."

Frank told Chaplain Bindell he wanted to leave his position as field nurse and "strike a blow" for the Union cause. The man listened with sympathy. Chaplain Bindell said a Federal spy had just been captured and executed at Richmond. He asked if Thompson would consider "a situation of great danger and of vast responsibility."

Private Thompson said *yes*. According to Sarah Emma's memoir, Chaplain Bindell recommended Private Thompson as a patriot and a good candidate to be a federal spy. Thompson was called to headquarters and interviewed. With unintended irony, Sarah Emma wrote that a "phrenological examination" was done, "finding that my organs of secretiveness, combativeness, etc. were largely developed."

Evidently, a physical examination was dispensed with in favor of phrenology—a "science" using measurements of the shape and dimensions of the skull to determine everything from intelligence to libido to the ability to carry a tune. Phrenologists believed each section of the brain controlled "organs" linking the mind and brain.

This "science" was the target of ridicule and jokes in the mid-nineteenth century. Journalist Ambrose Bierce defined phrenology as "the science of picking one's pocket through the brain . . . finding the organ one is a dupe with."

Whether Sarah Emma agreed with Bierce, she didn't say. She did, however, escape the physical examination that would have revealed her long-kept secret. And perhaps, that very secret was the source of her success in her next adventure.

Within a week Frank was dispatched to Fort Monroe. There he disguised himself as "contraband," a fugitive slave. He purchased a wig and a suit of homespun "slave cloth" and had his curly hair cropped short.

Frank used nitrate of silver to darken his skin. At night he crossed to rebel lines. The next morning he presented himself as "Ned," a free black man in search of employment. The Confederate soldiers put him to work digging trenches.

"Ned" was able to count the enemy's mounted guns, assess troop numbers, and sketch the layout of rebel lines. Then, Ned recognized a peddler who sold goods to Union troops. As recorded in Sarah's memoirs, Ned saw the traitor draw a map of the "entire works of General McClelland's position."

After three days of blister-raising work, "Ned" escaped back to the Union lines, taking a rebel rifle with him. The intelligence Frank took to General McClellan was valuable. A few weeks later, Private Thompson again crossed rebel lines; this time as "Bridget," an Irish peddler woman.

So, Sarah Emma was pretending to be Frank. Frank, in turn, was pretending to be Bridget. The fascinating, though convoluted, tale nearly unravels in the telling.

"Bridget" was waylaid by a bout of malaria. She took shelter in an abandoned shack only to find a dying Confederate soldier there. Although the Confederate was an enemy, Frank felt morally obligated to care for the dying man with kindness. Then, as "Bridget," Frank used the dead man's identification to gain entry to the Confederate camp. "Bridget" stayed long enough to learn the location of every hidden cannon and regiment along the Chickahominy swamp.

Some scholars think Sarah Emma's memoirs reported her years as a soldier as she wished to recall them, not as they actually occurred. While Frank's service is documented, the veracity of narratives in Sarah Emma's memoir has been questioned. For example, Sarah Emma wrote that after the Battle of Antietam, she found a wounded soldier who, before death, confessed she was a woman. According to Edmonds's memoir, the woman claimed to have enlisted with her brother, who had died that very day. At the dying soldier's request, "Frank" buried her sister-in-uniform, ensuring that the woman's secret would never be discovered.

As part of the Army of the Potomac, Private Thompson and the 2nd Michigan fought in major battles. Some, like Bull Run and the battle at Fredericksburg, were Union defeats. Every battle was a slaughter on one side or both. Frank's tour of duty as a spy was limited to a few forays behind enemy lines while most of his time was spent nursing wounded men.

Although her memoir often romanticized the spiritual beauty of patriots dying with faith in God, Sarah Emma wrote graphic descriptions of the terrible suffering she witnessed.

Thompson suffered from malaria. In Sarah Emma's memoir, she wrote that ongoing illness, coupled with the horrible scenes of death and suffering she'd witnessed, shattered her emotionally. She wrote, "I could do nothing but weep hour after hour. . . . All the horrid scenes that I had witnessed . . . I could think of nothing else."

Sarah Emma wrote that this emotional collapse and physical illness were so debilitating that the surgeon "made out a certificate of disability and I was forthwith released from further duty . . . in the Federal army."

In April of 1863 the 2nd Michigan received orders sending them to Mississippi under command of Gen. Ulysses S. Grant. On April 19, Private Frank Thompson was missing at roll call. He was classified as a deserter.

The circumstances under which Frank Thompson left the 2nd Michigan are open to debate. In one interview Sarah Emma said she was ill with malaria and feared her secret would be discovered. Forced to choose between desertion and discovery, she chose desertion.

During Frank's sojourn with the 2nd Michigan, he met Jerome Robbins. Frank revealed his true identity to this close friend. Robbins, it seems, kept the secret that Frank was actually a woman. Then, Frank deserted. Robbins recorded this in his diary and mentioned intense feelings of betrayal and shock.

Sarah Emma went to Oberlin, Ohio. She continued to dress as a man until her health returned. Then, taking her true name and identity again, she wrote her memoir, *Unsexed, or the Female Soldier.* To Edmonds's credit, she donated profits from this very successful book to soldiers' aid and volunteered with the Christian Commission hospital at Harpers Ferry until the war's end.

In 1867 Sarah Emma married Linas Seely. She discarded her first name and left her mark on Linas's family name by adding a final *e*. So, her fifth and final identity became S. Emma Edmonds Seelye.

Emma and Linas lost three children to death. They adopted two sons. In 1869 they moved to Charlevoix, Michigan. Linas's skill as a mechanic was sound, but his business abilities were limited. They moved often, living in at least seven states during their thirty-one-year marriage.

In 1884 Emma attended a reunion of the 2nd Michigan Infantry in Flint. She shocked everyone by introducing herself as "Frank." Then, and for the remainder of her life, Emma suffered from malaria. The 2nd Michigan veterans managed to overcome their shock and encouraged Emma, in light of this illness, to apply for a veteran's pension.

Emma launched a letter-writing campaign to Washington. Members of the 2nd Michigan wrote on her behalf. She obtained a pension and petitioned to have the word "deserter" removed from her military record. In late 1884 Emma was granted a monthly pension of twelve dollars. One year later her record was cleared of desertion charges, and she received back pay and bounties.

In the 1890s Linas and Emma moved to Texas. In 1893 their son Charles followed his mother by enlisting in Company H of the Michigan 33rd Volunteer Infantry. Emma joined the George B. McClellan Post of the Grand Army of the Republic (GAR), becoming the only woman admitted to that veterans organization.

Repeated bouts of malaria eroded Emma's health. This adventurous woman was unable to travel and spent much of her time reading and corresponding with friends. She died on September 5, 1898, at age fifty-seven, and was buried with full military honors at the GAR cemetery in Houston. Her official epitaph read, EMMA E. SEELYE, ARMY NURSE.

ANNA HOWARD SHAW

1847-1919

Pioneer, Preacher, Political Activist

"I WAS BORN IN NEWCASTLE-ON-TYNE, ENGLAND, OF Scottish parents on the fourteenth day of February, 1847. . . . Forced into bankruptcy two years before my birth . . . my father began to dream the great dream of those days, he would go to America."

Thus begins Anna Howard Shaw's 1915 autobiography, *The Story of a Pioneer,* tracing her life from that dramatic arrival in America as a four-year-old, through her days as a young pioneer in Michigan, to her adulthood as a scholar, activist, and leader.

Thomas Shaw, his wife, Nicolas, and their family immigrated to America in 1851. In 1859 they left Lawrence, Massachusetts, headed for what Anna called in her memoir the "great, northwestern" wilderness. Thomas was, as his daughter aptly described him, a dreamer. He was motivated by a dream of establishing a colony of like-minded, progressive people in a rural utopia. Neither Thomas nor his friends knew anything about farming. However, they were undaunted, and the Shaws relocated in northwestern Michigan. The nearest town was Paris. Today Paris is a small-town, rural community. In 1859, it was a spot on a map surrounded by forests.

ANNA HOWARD SHAW

While her father dreamed, Anna Shaw and her family struggled to survive. Anna's father and twenty-year-old brother James preceded the rest of the family to Michigan. The two men, who knew little or nothing about building, found land and erected a shell of a cabin. Anna later described it in her memoir, charitably, as "ramshackle." Thomas returned to Massachusetts and his paying job. James stayed behind. A few months later, Nicolas and the four youngest children joined James in Michigan. Thomas and the two older boys remained in Massachusetts for eighteen months. Although Thomas sent money, he had, for all practical purposes, abandoned his wife with twenty-year-old James, one slightly younger daughter, and children ages eight, ten, and twelve.

As an adult, Anna Howard Shaw recalled the trip to Michigan in detail. They traveled by train to Grand Rapids, which was then a small city near the Lake Michigan shore. James met them in a wagon with a "horrible resemblance to a vehicle from the health department." This wagon, crammed with bedding and provisions, wasn't big enough for the family, so the children walked much of the one hundred miles to their homestead.

It took the family seven days to reach their land. Thomas had painted a rosy picture of a farm in a beautiful, wild area. Instead they found the "four walls and the roof of a good-sized log house . . . its doors and windows represented by the square holes, its floor also a thing of the future." Anna wrote in her memoir, "I shall never forget the look my mother turned upon the place."

Nicolas stood in the empty doorway without speaking. She sank to the ground, buried her face in her hands, and sat in silence for hours. Anna's memoir exposed raw emotion as she wrote, "Our little world had crumbled under our feet. Never before had we seen our mother give way to despair."

Thus began difficult years for Anna Howard Shaw. The next morning, when James and the children held a family council, Anna took the role of an adult. The immediate needs were to construct doors and windows. They built a crude loft. Nicolas was well enough to sew. Eleanor and Mary, the older sisters, did the cooking, washing, and cleaning. James, Anna, and eight-year-old Harry chopped firewood. They felled trees. They gathered wild fruit. Harry became an expert fisherman. Lacking hooks or traps, the three fashioned snares using wires from the girls' hoop skirts.

Shaw's memoir softens the terrible reality. The cow died. Their only help came from a bachelor farmer who lived eighteen miles away, and the family was in real danger of freezing to death during that first winter. Shaw merely mentioned "increasing difficulty as the temperature steadily fell."

Later, she wrote more frankly. "Like most men, my dear father should never have married. Though his nature was one of the sweetest I have ever known . . . in practical matters he remained to the end of his days, as irresponsible as a child. . . . When my father took up his claim . . . and sent my mother and five young children to live there alone, he gave no thought to the manner in which we were to make the struggle and survive . . . we lacked not only every comfort, but even the bare necessities of life."

About three months after the family's arrival, James became very ill and returned to Massachusetts for surgery. Although James survived the surgery, he never returned to Michigan. Nicolas's depression deepened, and all outside work fell to Anna and Harry. Anna took on tasks far beyond the normal expectation for a thirteen-year-old.

After James's departure the family's greatest challenge was surviving the winter. When the creek froze, they melted snow for water. Come spring, Anna decided they must have a well, and their neighbor, the young bachelor, helped with this daunting task. Anna wrote, "When we had dug as far as we could reach with our spades, my assistant descended into the hole and threw the earth up to an edge, from which I, in turn, removed it." They continued in this way, with the young man tossing dirt from the well's bottom to a ledge halfway to the top. Anna stood on this narrow ledge and threw dirt with a shovel onto the land above. In the end buckets of dirt were handed from the young man to Anna.

The children spent the winter and their little free time the rest of the year reading and rereading books brought from Massachusetts. It was in this isolated cabin that Anna read histories of Greece and Rome. She and Harry worked their way through arithmetic and algebra. Anna read and loved *Uncle Tom's Cabin.* Her parents were abolitionists and had on at least one occasion given sanctuary to a fugitive slave. *Uncle Tom's Cabin* had great impact on Anna. When her father finally joined the family, bringing more books, Anna wrote in her memoir that she fell on them "as a starving man falls upon food."

Thomas's return, along with sons Jack and Tom, brought help to the family. Anna, however, found scant appreciation from her father. This, too, she recorded honestly in her memoir. She wrote of one incident when she lost track of time while reading in the woods, her father called her an "idler who wasted time while mother labored." He said she was lazy and would make nothing of herself.

Anna was deeply hurt. When her father's tirade ended, she replied, "Father, some day I am going to college. And before I die, I shall be worth ten thousand dollars."

To Anna this was more money than she could imagine any woman ever earning. She had secretly dreamed of being a preacher. She wanted to give hope to people and teach them about goodness and God. At that moment, facing her father's ridicule, Anna set her mind to this dream.

The growing state of Michigan required communities to establish public schools. Still, Anna was nearly fourteen when a school finally opened near Paris. She enrolled, though it soon became apparent that she was both more capable and well-read than the young, barely trained teacher.

At age fifteen Anna passed the examination and was hired to teach in a new school at the pay of two dollars a week and board. She had no training and was expected to simply pass on the content she had learned, with or without textbooks and supplies. She "boarded round" with families of her pupils. Anna wrote in her memoir, "The first year I had about fourteen pupils, of varying ages, sizes, and temperaments, and there was hardly a book in the school-room except those I owned."

In April 1862 the Civil War began. President Lincoln called for troops, and the men of Paris, Michigan, responded. Jack enlisted, and Tom, though still a young teenager, became a Union bugle boy. Not long after, Thomas once again abandoned his wife and family. He volunteered for the Union cause and served until the end of the war.

With her father's absence, Anna nearly gave up. Her mother's depression deepened. Her sister Eleanor died in childbirth, leaving the child in Anna's care. The family made ends meet by taking in boarders, making and selling quilts, and, for Anna, teaching.

Anna wrote in her memoir, "I was walking seven and eight miles a day, and doing extra work before and after school hours . . . It was an incessant struggle to keep our land, to pay our taxes, and to live . . ." For more than three years, Anna kept the family from bankruptcy. Sometimes her teacher's salary—never more than six dollars a week—was their only income.

Finally, the Civil War ended. "The end of the Civil War brought freedom to me, too," Anna Shaw reflected in her memoir. When her father and brothers returned, she began to save money for a long-treasured, almost abandoned dream: college.

Shaw quit teaching and moved to Big Rapids with her married sister. Since employment options for women were few and low paying, she decided to learn a trade and save money for college.

A few weeks after Shaw's arrival in Big Rapids, a novel event occurred. A female minister, the Reverend Marianna Thompson, preached at the Unitarian church. Shaw was enthralled. "It was a wonderful moment," she recalled in her memoir, "when I saw my first woman minister enter her pulpit; and as I listened to her sermon, thrilled to my soul, all my early aspirations to become a minister myself stirred in me . . ."

Reverend Thompson advised Shaw to forget about learning a trade. "Go to school," she said. "You can't do anything until you have an education. Get it, and get it now."

Shaw enrolled in Big Rapids High School's college preparatory course. She determined to stay "as long as my money held out." In Big Rapids High School, Anna met the first of many women friends and mentors.

The high school "preceptress" was Lucy Foot, a graduate of Albion College. When Shaw confided her dream of being a minister to Miss Foot, the woman guided her to public speaking and debate classes. She introduced Shaw to Dr. Peck, a leader in the Methodist Church, where a movement was under way to license women to preach.

Elder Peck asked Shaw to preach at the quarterly meeting of the Methodist Church. Miss Foot encouraged and guided her, but as she prepared, Shaw was haunted by the knowledge that her family would not support her. In fact her sister Mary begged her to give up the idea. The family thought a female preacher would be a blot on their reputation. When Shaw said she couldn't refuse God's calling, her sister withdrew in silence.

The quarterly meeting, with Anna Shaw preaching, was a great success. Her family, however, expressed their disapproval. Her father even offered to pay for college at prestigious University of Michigan at Ann Arbor if Anna would abandon her plans to preach. Anna was tempted. She longed to learn and she longed to become a minister. At last she decided; she told her family, "I will go my solitary way."

After graduation, Shaw entered Albion College, a progressive school in Michigan. She supported herself by preaching and speaking on temperance. In her memoir she wrote of one preaching assignment in 1874 that challenged her resilience and grit. Shaw agreed to preach at a lumber camp while the pastor was away on his honeymoon. She traveled twenty-two miles by stage to Seberwing, Michigan. From there, the only way to reach the camp was to hire a driver and wagon able to navigate through densely wooded terrain.

After some effort she found a willing driver. They set off that night in the dark. Shaw felt uncomfortable. The man seemed rough and unpleasant. He began to tell horrifying stories of lumber camps and "stockades" in the wilderness. He cursed and said he was no fool, he knew "what kind of woman" would drive alone into the woods with him. Then, he stopped the wagon. Shaw was terrified. She opened her satchel and placed her hand on the revolver she carried inside. She drew out the gun and placed its barrel against his back. *"Drive!"* she commanded. "If you stop again, or speak, I'll shoot you."

They reached the lumber camp after more terror-filled hours and, the following morning, Shaw preached. The building was packed with lumbermen, and the offering was the largest ever taken. But Shaw discovered the attendance and generosity of the men had nothing to do with spiritual hunger. Evidently, the driver had told his friends about the "woman minister who carried a revolver," and the whole camp had poured into town to see her.

In February 1876 Shaw packed her few possessions and moved to Boston to begin theological studies at Boston University. In *The Story of a Pioneer*, she wrote, "My class at the theological school was composed of forty-two young men and my unworthy self," and "women theologians paid heavily for the privilege of being women."

Students who were licensed preachers received free room and inexpensive board at a "club" established for divinity students, but although Shaw was a licensed preacher, she was barred from the club's dining facilities and given two dollars a week to rent a room outside the school. She struggled to feed herself with occasional income from speaking or preaching.

Shaw received no help from her family. At one point she was eating only "crackers and milk." Eventually, a "benefactor" anonymously gave her $3.50 a week. With this support Anna continued until graduation.

Once she was done with school, Shaw was hired by a church in East Dennis, on nearby Cape Cod. She found a divided church and bitter people, and it took two years to heal the rifts and set this church on a better course.

The skills she learned in East Dennis were needed when Shaw applied for ordination in the Methodist Church. Although Anna Shaw and one other woman, Anna Oliver, were examined at length by the conference board and declared fit for ordination, the bishop refused to accept their names. He discounted their years of study, Anna's leadership in East Dennis, and her graduation from Boston University.

Anna Shaw sought ordination in the Methodist Protestant denomination. That, too, resulted in a battle about gender. At the conference meeting in Tarrytown, New York, heated debate surrounded the question of ordaining a woman. In the end Shaw's ordination was accepted.

Shaw returned to East Dennis as pastor. In 1882 she decided to attend medical school. In 1885 she graduated from Boston Medical School and began work in Boston's slums.

Although Shaw didn't intend to leave pastoral ministry for medicine, she noted in her memoir the need to add medical skill to her "mental equipment." Shaw's part-time medical practice was the only medical care for many "women of the streets," and she performed surgeries and delivered babies while still a pastor in East Dennis.

For one year Shaw juggled both jobs. Then in late 1885 she resigned as pastor to join the Massachusetts Women's Suffrage Association as a lecturer and organizer. Although Shaw was deeply committed to the suffrage association's work, the salary offered was meager. Shaw's memoir notes that when she requested more money, she was "reminded this was a good salary for a woman."

Shaw had to make a stand for her principles. A "good salary *for a woman*" was, she judged, not a good salary for a self-supporting individual. She quit the suffrage association and launched a career as a freelance lecturer and speaker. In the first month she earned three hundred dollars. She quickly became a sought-after public speaker on temperance and women's suffrage.

For three years Shaw spoke on the lecture circuit. Then, in 1888 Susan B. Anthony persuaded her that winning women the right to vote would be the key to temperance reform, and Shaw made the life-changing decision to join Anthony and the National American Woman Suffrage Association (NAWSA). For the next eighteen years, Shaw and Anthony worked shoulder to shoulder for the right to vote for women. Yet, Shaw remained, first and foremost, a preacher. She continued to speak about God and goodness, hoping to change people's hearts. Shaw became Susan B. Anthony's co-leader and an important leader in her own right. The two traveled extensively in the West, educating, speaking, and convincing men and women alike of the need for women's suffrage.

Shaw entered full-time suffrage work during a tumultuous time. Suffrage organizers in England were becoming increasingly radicalized, even executing organized acts of civil disobedience and destruction of property. Some American suffragists wanted to follow their lead. Shaw and the "old guard" refused. Conflict about this and other issues threatened to break the movement.

After Anthony's retirement in 1900, Shaw became vice president, then president, of the National American Woman Suffrage

Association. She provided needed leadership, and in 1906 she conducted the funeral service for her dear friend and colleague, Susan B. Anthony.

During her tenure with the NAWSA, the suffrage movement was repeatedly betrayed by politicians and parties. From 1911 until 1916 Shaw threw herself into efforts to get Congress to pass the Equal Rights Amendment. Starting in January 1917, women stood silently outside the White House every day, holding signs demanding the right to vote. The ongoing demonstration ended with the beginning of World War I later that year.

At the start of World War I, with women still denied the right to vote, Shaw was offered and accepted the chair of the Women's Committee of the Council of National Defense. This committee was formed to organize the work and resources of women across the country in support of the war effort. Many historians theorize that the federal government's motivation in creating the committee was to placate women and distract them from suffrage efforts.

The committee had no real power. However, Shaw had never been stopped by the failure of those in power to share it. She and her committee, including Carrie Chapman Catt, another former president of NAWSA, achieved amazing impact for disenfranchised women assigned to what men in power considered a token appointment.

The Women's Committee marshaled tens of thousands of volunteers across the country. Fund-raisers for everything from medical supplies to support for returning veterans netted millions of dollars. Under Shaw's leadership the Women's Committee became a force to be reckoned with. By the war's end the groundwork was laid for an official, funded, and staffed women's "field division" of the Council of National Defense.

After World War I, Catt and others returned to the suffrage struggle. Shaw began a national tour, speaking for ratification of the

League of Nations. During the tour Shaw contracted pneumonia. She died on July 2, 1919, in her Moylan, Pennsylvania, home.

At her death, Anna Howard Shaw was among a handful of ordained American woman ministers. She had helped shape the suffrage movement. Two months prior to her death, she had received the national Distinguished Service Medal for her work with the Women's Committee.

However, like her colleagues Susan B. Anthony and Elizabeth Cady Stanton, Anna Howard Shaw did not live to see the passage of the Nineteenth Amendment to the Constitution, giving the women of America the right to vote.

REBECCA SHELLEY

1887-1984

Peacemaker

"FELIX RATHMER WAS AN ARDENT WOOER . . . He took me on the rebound and I took him on faith," Rebecca Shelley wrote in her 1961 memoir, *A Widow's Mite,* dedicated to her husband, Felix.

Rebecca Shelley, a pacifist, political activist, and ardent feminist, had returned to Battle Creek, Michigan, at the end of World War I. She was supporting herself by writing and publishing a newspaper for the poultry industry when she met Felix Rathmer, a German war-resister. When Rathmer had been conscripted into Kaiser Wilhelm's army, he had fled and gone underground. And, with borders being more permeable in 1922 than today, Rathmer emigrated by simply walking off a ship anchored in New York harbor.

Rebecca Shelley was a peace activist. Rathmer, a romantic. Within a month of meeting, the two married. After their Yellowstone honeymoon, Shelley discovered that, according to the Expatriation Act of 1907, women marrying non-U.S. citizens forfeited citizenship. She returned from her honeymoon as a woman with no country. A new law called the Equal Nationality Law had been

REBECCA SHELLEY

passed to remedy this discrimination against women. However, it would become effective six weeks after Shelley and Rathmer married.

Felix and Rebecca assumed that her repatriation simply would require the filling out of forms. They were wrong. Repatriation required a pledge to the United States of America, including the question, "If necessary, are you willing to bear arms in defense of this country?" Shelley's answer was *no*. And, for the next twenty-two years, she battled the United States government for her right to be both a citizen and a pacifist.

Rebecca Shelley's life was, in many ways, a battle of conscience and her conviction that humanity was to be valued above nations.

In 1887 Rebecca was born in Sugar Valley, Pennsylvania, the fourth of eleven children. As a young woman, Rebecca changed her family name from Shelly to Shelley to reflect her love of the British poet. In an autobiographical outline written in the early 1980s, Rebecca describes her mother as a "strong character, musically gifted" and her father as a "fond companion, [and] fascinating storyteller." Mrs. Shelly raised the children. Mr. Shelly was, in turn, a blacksmith, farmer, teacher, and minister.

Nowhere in this brief autobiographical sketch does Shelley mention her parents' names.

A biographer, Janet Reedy, wrote, "Rebecca's inheritance from her father was his charm. From her mother she got determination, stick-to-itiveness, and stubbornness."

The Shelly family was religious, though not pacifists. Mother was the family disciplinarian, and she plied the "switch" somewhat liberally. Father often found time to spend with his eleven children individually, telling stories and roaming in nature. As an adult, Rebecca's temperament reflected those of both parents.

The Shellys valued education, and their sons and daughters attended college. Rebecca and her sister Laura attended Clarion Normal, where they were provided minimal training in *what* to teach and even less in *how* to teach it.

At age seventeen, after two years of study, Rebecca took her first teaching position. She fell back on the refuge of the fearful—rigid control. Afraid her students would run away, she refused to let them leave class to use the bathroom. Once, she whipped a defiant sixteen-year-old with a fire shovel.

While Rebecca was teaching, her heart was elsewhere. Back at Clarion State, she'd heard a chapel speaker tell how she'd worked her way through college. So when her father was offered a pastorate in Michigan, Rebecca set her sails toward Ann Arbor and the University of Michigan.

Rebecca's father wanted her to attend a small religious school where her faith would be supported rather than challenged. Rebecca, on the other hand, knew what she wanted and was determined.

Rebecca was accepted at the University of Michigan and worked her way through school. She boarded with a professor's family, trading domestic work for room and board. For a year she ate her meals alone in that family's kitchen.

After three years in Ann Arbor, Rebecca earned a bachelor's degree in German. She was elected to Phi Beta Kappa, a national society honoring students with top academic performance.

During Rebecca's senior year at the university, Jane Addams, a social reformer and leader in the new field of social work, was invited to address students on the subject of women's suffrage. However, the administration decided Addams's subject was too controversial and barred her from campus. Rebecca Shelley and many other women students were outraged. For Rebecca it marked the beginning of a lifelong, increasingly radical, commitment to social justice.

Rebecca's first job was as a high school German teacher in Hayward, Wisconsin. It was 1910. As a University of Michigan Phi Beta Kappa graduate, had she been a man, she would have chosen from among many well-paying employment opportunities. As a woman, she was fortunate to be hired at eighty dollars a month in a rural school.

Yet, Shelley was determined to succeed. She set a goal of heading the high school German department, a position of authority unavailable to women in that era.

On a summer trip to Germany with friends Will and Maria Worrell, Rebecca met Franz Willman, a literature and music critic for a Leipzig newspaper. The two became friends and traveling companions. At the end of their travels, Franz proposed. Rebecca couldn't accept. She couldn't say no. She asked for more time.

During the next two years, Franz and Rebecca corresponded. Shelley taught one more year in Hayward and another in Everett, Washington. Then in 1913 she accepted Franz's proposal and returned to Germany to meet his family and announce their engagement formally.

Rebecca desperately wanted to impress the Willman family. Two years earlier she had met Franz's mother, who had seemed unimpressed with the young American girl. This time Rebecca prepared her trousseau carefully and rehearsed what she would say to Franz's mother. Arriving in Leipzig, she descended the steps of the train and promptly fainted.

Politics interrupted Rebecca and Franz's wedding plans. In August 1914, war was declared in Europe. Franz was called to active military duty. Rebecca, who had quit her job, returned to the United States.

In Freeport, Illinois, Rebecca found work as a writer. Eager for intelligent company, she joined a women's club. At the club Rebecca engaged in a debate about American military presence in the world. The debate opened doors for Rebecca to new intellectual territory. She corresponded with Jane Addams, a Freeport native and outspoken pacifist. She learned that Addams and other feminist and pacifist women from America and Europe were planning an international women's congress at The Hague, in the Netherlands, hoping to influence European governments to end the war.

At that time, American women weren't even granted the right to vote. Addams and her fellows were engaging in a truly David-and-Goliath battle. Women planned to confront governments comprised completely of powerful men. Rebecca decided she must go, too.

Rebecca sold her wedding trousseau to purchase passage to New York and then to Europe. In a moment's decision, she changed her life direction. She would spend the next weeks surrounded by brilliant, activist women committed to women's suffrage and peace. Rebecca's real education as a woman was to begin.

The International Women's Congress based its work on two goals: gaining the vote for women in every nation and using that political influence of millions of voting women to bring about peace. They believed the first would naturally lead to the second.

At The Hague the American women were joined by their counterparts from across Europe. The delegates from England were absent because the British government had refused to allow them to attend.

At the conference a plan was endorsed proposing neutral mediation to end the war. Developed by Julia Grace Wales, a professor at the University of Wisconsin at Madison, the plan required representatives to visit the heads of state of both warring and neutral European nations. It was an ambitious vision made more challenging by the fact that these representatives would be women.

Following the conference, women did present their plan for peace to leaders across Europe. Usually, they were courteously received and, just as courteously, their words and vision were ignored.

Rebecca put her German language skills to work as an interpreter for Angela Morgan, a writer and delegate from the United States. In Germany the two met officials and private citizens. Angela conducted interviews and gathered information for articles she wrote and wired back to American newspapers. At the time, Germany wanted U.S. support, so Angela and Rebecca were made welcome.

In Munich a German professor learned that Rebecca's fiancé was an officer in the German army. To Rebecca's shock and delight, the man arranged leave for Franz so he could spend a few days with her in his home country. The reunion was bittersweet. The couple had been separated for two years. They were thrilled to be together. However, during those two years both had changed. Franz was an active-duty military officer in a country on the edge of war. Rebecca was a newly hatched young pacifist, trying her political and philosophical wings.

Franz was a patriot. He disliked the "German emperor" and was personally unsupportive of the war. However, he also believed in German honor.

Rebecca returned her engagement ring. Franz convinced her to keep it. The couple parted with great pain and confusion. They were in love, but the war threatened to destroy their relationship. Rebecca never saw Franz again. He would die of encephalitis before the war's end.

Rebecca and Angela Morgan returned to Michigan. They lived on savings, borrowed money, and cash from pawned jewelry, holding street meetings in Detroit where Rebecca spoke about the need for peace and the potential hope of neutral mediation. Morgan dressed in white, reciting her poem "The Battle Cry of Mothers."

The pair hoped to make contact with Henry Ford, a wealthy Detroit businessman. Ford had publicly called the war a "waste of men and resources." He said he would give his fortune to end the war. Rebecca and Angela hoped to convince him that neutral mediation was the best vehicle by which peace could be obtained.

Angela returned to New York. Rebecca did meet Henry and Clara Ford. She was accompanied by Rosika Schwimmer, a

Hungarian pacifist and antiwar activist touring the United States with the message of neutral mediation.

During the meeting Rebecca took advantage of a moment alone with Clara Ford to ask for ten thousand dollars for a campaign to reach President Woodrow Wilson with telegrams from every corner of the country urging him to support a national conference on neutral mediation. To Rebecca's surprise Mrs. Ford agreed. On the spot Clara Ford lifted her skirt and slipped a change purse from the top of her stocking. She handed Rebecca thirty dollars as a good-faith symbol of her commitment to the proposal.

Rebecca Shelley was pulled into a whirlwind. When President Wilson refused to consider neutral mediation, Henry Ford took up the cause himself. He chartered a ship to Europe and invited influential Americans of all persuasions to join him. He publicly declared the purpose of "Ford's Peace Ship" voyage was to bring America's "boys out of the trenches by Christmas."

What had begun as the dream and efforts of a coalition of women committed to peace and neutral mediation quickly became Henry Ford's own version of political action. Ford simply took over. Neutral mediation was lost as a focus. Some women leaders withdrew from the project. Some remained, thinking that some impact was better than none.

"Ford's Peace Ship" was a failure at best and a laughingstock at worst. The voyage did little for peace. It did serve to bring Rebecca into the center of the antiwar effort among American women.

Soon after the Peace Ship fiasco, the Unites States entered the war. Suddenly, work for peace was painted as unpatriotic. As the movement disintegrated, Rebecca learned of Franz Willman's death. Within weeks Rebecca lost her life purpose and her first love. She grieved alone. Franz was buried across an ocean, and Rebecca would never know whether she and her sweetheart could have worked out their differences and married happily.

Rebecca fell into a deep depression. In 1917 she returned to Michigan, seeking help for her depression at the Battle Creek Sanitarium, a spa owned by health-activist and antiwar-activist Dr. John Harvey Kellogg. After a few months of rest, she moved in with her sister and brother-in-law on their Three Rivers farm. It was a terrible time. Rebecca was still depressed and still mourning Franz. She learned she was under investigation by the FBI for her antiwar work. Her brother-in-law wanted her and her radical thinking out of his house.

During the next year Rebecca's healing and restoration began. She read *Lay Down Your Arms,* a novel by Austrian baroness and antiwar activist Bertha von Suttner, the first woman to receive the Nobel Peace Prize.

The novel rekindled Rebecca's passion and clarity of vision. Americans needed a voice like von Suttner's, she decided. She determined to be that voice. Rebecca decided to write what Janet Reedy described as "the Uncle Tom's Cabin of the peace movement."

As a means to become self-supporting, Rebecca bought a newspaper called the *Michigan Poultry Breeder.* She moved to Battle Creek and dined each evening at the Bernard McFadden Physical Culture Institute, a health spa begun by faddist and entrepreneur Bernard McFadden. It was there that she met Felix Rathmer, a young German engineer who was vacationing at the institute.

Shelley and Rathmer married. At first, the young couple fashioned their own version of a bicoastal marriage. Felix returned to Youngstown and his job. Rebecca remained in Battle Creek, planning to sell the newspaper and join her husband. Instead, Felix couldn't bear the separation. He quit his job, and the couple invested the profit from the sale of Rebecca's business to start Rathmer Electric Company.

Rathmer was a skilled engineer. Rebecca was conscripted as bookkeeper and office girl. They bought a farm on a lake near

Battle Creek and built a combination office and apartment in town. The business grew, but Rebecca had no time for writing or peace work.

Then, 1929 brought the collapse of the American stock market. As the Depression tightened its grip, Felix and Rebecca lost their business. Only assistance from a Home Owners Loan Corporation saved their farm. Rebecca found work with the Federal Writers' Project, interviewing ethnic minorities in Detroit. Felix was hired in Texas. Ongoing separations and relocations strained their marriage.

During this time Rebecca was still denied her American citizenship. In 1931 she filed for repatriation and was denied when she refused to promise to defend the nation by force of arms. She would refile and appear in court four times before, in 1944, her petition to regain her citizenship was finally accepted.

At the start of World War II, Rebecca Shelley was still fighting for repatriation. She held back from active antiwar actions, fearing that the government might deport Felix as retribution for her refusal to affirm willingness to bear arms.

In 1959 Felix suffered a fatal heart attack. Rebecca blamed herself, telling friends that she should have understood that symptoms of tiredness and chest and arm pain signaled more than a need for rest. Rebecca was seventy-one years old. Some friends expected her to settle into quiet widowhood. They were mistaken.

In 1954, five years before Felix's death, Rebecca had written then-President Dwight Eisenhower expressing grave concern about U.S. policy in an area of the world about which few Americans were even aware: Vietnam. The United States was considering sending troops to "stabilize" Vietnam. Rebecca warned that war would result. She was right.

By the mid-1960s, the "conflict" in Vietnam had become a full-fledged war. American and Vietnamese soldiers died by the thousands. At some point, Rebecca symbolized those deaths by wearing "widow's weeds," a long black dress and veil. Dressed for mourning, she began solo peace vigils.

In 1964 she was nominated as a peace party candidate for vice president. She conducted a seven-day silent vigil at the Tomb of the Unknown Soldier in Arlington National Cemetery. For six days she stood in silence. On the seventh, two companions unrolled a banner. They were immediately surrounded by military guards who confiscated the banner and forced the women to leave.

In 1965 Alice Herz, a close friend of Shelley's, burned herself to death on a Detroit street corner to protest U.S. involvement in Vietnam. Shelley was deeply affected. At the age of eighty, she launched a world peace tour. She visited nonaligned nations, pleading, once again, for neutral mediation to bring an end to yet another war.

In each country she held silent vigils, praying for peace and making a public statement against her own nation's actions in Vietnam.

Returning to the United States, Rebecca continued her vigils. She kept vigil for weeks outside the post office in her Battle Creek home. She traveled to Washington, D.C., where, day after day, she bore silent witness at the White House gates, displaying a sign saying, STOP THE CRIME IN VIETNAM.

Before her death in 1984 at age ninety-seven, Shelley dreamed of a center for peace on her Battle Creek farm. Peaceways, though still largely a dream when Shelley died, was a gathering place for like-minded people. However, in the end, she sold all but ten acres of this land to finance peace missions.

In 1976 Shelley received the International Women's Year citation for her efforts for world peace. In 1979 the state of Michigan named her a Michigan International Citizen.

During her lifetime, Rebecca Shelley wrote *In Mourning for the War Dead, A Widow's Mite,* and *Je M'Accuse* (the latter meaning "I

Confess" and penned in Paris during the Vietnam War). Her books combine personal history, reflections, and poetry.

Rebecca Shelley's poetry reflects her commitment to peace. She closed *A Widow's Mite* with the following words:

Let the war-ravaged people speak. . . .
No more Hiroshimas. . . .
No more Warsaw Massacres. . . .

Oh martyred Lidice! Bleeding Poland!
Beautiful Dresden no one could save.
Nor art nor pity nor the Madonna's hovering angels.
Hearts broken at Stalingrad! Pearl Harbor!
The beaches of Normandy!

Oh my people of all nations.
Brothers and sisters of one human family,
all stricken by war. . . .
Cry out your heart's anguish, my tears mingle with yours!
But cry out with one mighty voice to leaders and statesmen:
NO MORE WAR!

ANA CLEMENC

1888–1956

Holding the Union Banner in Calumet

In northern Michigan during the 1890s, the approach of a new century was marked by the arrival of thousands of immigrants seeking work in the copper mines. Some were Italian quarrymen or Cornish "Cousin Jacks." Finns came, with a dream of land and to escape the encroaching power of the Russian tsar. And a collection of "Austrians" came from the serf-nations of the Austro-Hungarian Empire to seek a life beyond the grinding poverty of Serbia, Croatia, Slovenia, or Macedonia. One of those immigrant families was the Klobuchars.

Born in 1888, Ana Klobuchar was the eldest child of a Slovenian miner and his wife. She grew up surrounded by miners and mining. When she was a child, in Calumet, Michigan, everyone she knew depended on the mines for a living. Her father toiled in the Red Jacket mine. Her mother made a few dollars doing cooking, laundry, or working as a midwife. Ana, herself, would complete eighth grade and follow in her mother's footsteps by marrying a miner.

By 1910 Ana and her husband, Joseph Clemenc, were living the miner's life in Calumet, home to some of the most profitable mines

STRIKING MINERS IN CALUMET

in the world. Men carved copper from shafts more than a mile deep. Although located in Michigan's Upper Peninsula, a relatively isolated area, Calumet boasted an opera house, a hospital, social halls, schools, and an electric streetcar.

The mines produced enormous wealth for their owners. Eastern investors made millions. The miners, however, risked their lives in unsafe conditions and lived "peda to peda," stretching their income from one payday until the next.

The Calumet and Hecla Mining Company (C&H) owned the mines. It also owned most judges, workers' houses, the schools the local children attended, and the stores where mining families bought their groceries. C&H controlled the police force and county government. Miners earned $2.50 a day. The mine manager, James Naughton, was paid $85,000 a year.

Historian Angus Murdock described the miners' life in his book, *Boom Copper,* "Your home was heated with coal brought on company boats. You washed in water from company pumps and had your dinner under company made electric lights. Even your garbage was carried in company wagons. . . . and your wife would have your children at the company hospital."

In this setting Joseph and Ana Clemenc lived and worked. Joseph Clemenc joined and became a leader in the Western Miners' Federation (WMF) union. Ana was a socialist by conviction and a strong advocate of workers' rights.

By 1913 tension between mine owners and workers was escalating. Mine bosses cheated workers who spoke little or no English. Owners refused to increase wages. To save money, owners adopted a one-man, stand-up drill. This meant a miner might operate a drill, alone, for twelve hours. Accidents were frequent. An injured man would have to be transported more than a mile back to the surface for medical attention. Miners began to call the drill the widow-maker. More and more miners joined the WMF.

By spring the word "strike" was in the air. By July union members consulted Western Miners' Federation officers. With WMF support, they voted to strike. The miners were hopeful. But, the mine owners were ready.

On the first day of the strike, miners stayed home. The next morning, shouting and shoving matches ensued between strikers and nonstriking miners. The owners used this minor conflict as justification to petition Michigan's governor, Woodbridge Ferris, for help. Ferris sent Gen. P. L. Abbey, the entire 2,565-men-strong state militia under his command, and three brass bands to Calumet.

C&H owners hired several hundred armed guards. Many of the guards were streetwise hoodlums from New York in the employ of Waddell-Mahon agency, a supplier of "guards" and "detectives" able and willing to use force to break the union.

Federation members responded by parading each morning from the Miners' Union Hall to the entrances of each of C&H's three mine shafts—Red Jacket, Blue Jacket, and Yellow Jacket. Joseph and other union leaders hoped this show of solidarity would discourage defectors and intimidate nonstriking and newly hired "scab" workers.

The miners marched in their best clothes, with the local Western Miners' Federation president at the lead and their wives and children alongside. The WMF often sent union organizers and activists to join the marchers, hoping to keep morale and focus strong. The strikers were once joined by "Mother Jones," a nationally known, pro-union, eighty-year-old firebrand. This encouraged the miners but served to increase the owners' anger and determination to break the union.

Each morning, at the head of the parade, marched a tall woman in her early twenties. It was Ana Clemenc, marching to support her husband and her whole community. Ana carried a hand-sewn, silk American flag. The story of Ana's role in the strike was told by newspaper reporters and recorded in union bulletins and official documents.

Ana was called "Big Annie" or "Tall Annie" by friends and neighbors. At more than six feet in height, she was an imposing woman.

The strike became a driving force in Ana's life. She embraced it as a source of hope for her family and community. Some mornings, she would carry the flag, bound to a heavy staff, for five or even ten miles around the city.

As the marches continued, week after week, the situation became increasingly desperate. Striking families had no money and little food. C&H's thugs and the Michigan militia members lashed out or responded to union actions with violence. One militia member rode his horse into the middle of a crowd of strikers, injuring a small child. On other occasions, Waddell-Mahon "guards" beat innocent citizens and intimidated anyone on the streets.

One morning Ana and union president Frank King were stopped by a group of armed "deputies," militia infantrymen holding bayoneted guns, and cavalrymen astride horses and carrying drawn sabers. Ana was carrying a flag. A cavalryman rode up to Annie and struck the staff with his saber, knocking it from her hands. The flag and staff clattered to the ground. A fellow marcher reached down to retrieve the flag, but he, too was knocked down. Another militiaman speared the flag with his saber while his horse trampled on the silk fabric.

Ana grabbed the staff and pulled the flag from under the horse's hooves. An infantryman pulled out a pistol and aimed it at Frank King and Ana. He demanded the flags. The men struck at Ana's arm and the staff.

"Kill me," Ana shouted. "But I won't move. If this flag will not protect me, then I will die with it."

Witnesses reported that the standoff ended only when several strikers pushed their way between Ana and the armed men.

Ana became a symbol of purpose and solidarity for the strikers. Such symbols were needed as the weeks wore on without a single conciliatory move on the part of the mine owners. Money, food, and tempers were getting tighter each day.

One morning Ana approached a miner who had decided to break ranks and return to work. "Oh George!" she cried. "You're not going to work are you? . . . Stick with us and we'll stick with you."

Ana cajoled and persuaded until George stepped from the line of miners waiting to enter the shaft.

Two C&H scabs approached. They pushed George toward the mine, mocking, "Coward, are you stopping because a woman told you not to go to work?" George pushed back. More strikebreakers approached, and in a few seconds, a full-blown fight ensued. Ana stood on the sidelines, yelling encouragement to George and letting everyone in earshot know that C&H strikebreakers were beating a man for wanting to support the strike.

General Abbey approached and demanded that Ana leave. The general and some men forced Ana into a car. "Annie, why don't you stay at home," Abbey demanded.

"I won't stay at home," Ana responded. "My work is here. Nobody can stop me. I'm going to keep at it until this strike is won for the workers."

Abbey and his men took her to the Calumet jail. It was Ana's first ride in an automobile, though not her first visit to the jail. Ana Clemenc was charged with assault and battery. The sheriff confined her to a cell until noon, when she was released on bond. That day she wrote an account of her experience, which was later submitted and published in the October 2 edition of the *Miners' Bulletin* under the title "A Woman's Story."

As summer turned to fall, the strike situation escalated. The C&H owners refused to negotiate with WMF officials or even to speak with anyone carrying a union membership card. Some strikers returned to work. The remaining miners became more and more discouraged. With discouragement, came frustration, anger, and violence.

One night five hired gunmen surrounded a striker's house. They fired through the windows, killing two men and injuring an infant. Later a deputy sheriff and a striker killed each other in nearby Hurontown. And in early December, strikers fired their guns into a boardinghouse in Plainsdale, killing three newly arrived scab workers from Canada.

As Christmas approached, strikers and their families despaired. Strikers were threatened with eviction by mine owners, who were also their landlords. Ana Clemenc and some other women formed the Women's Alliance. By begging for money and help from union families in other regions and even other states, they planned a Christmas party for the desolate, discouraged strikers and their families.

While these plans were forming, Houghton and Calumet merchants, frustrated by loss of income and angry at the killings at Plainsdale, organized a "Citizens' Alliance" to oppose the strike.

Formation of the Citizens' Alliance was nearly a deathblow to the strikers' solidarity. Until that time, grocers and other merchants had been willing to extend credit to strikers. Now merchants threatened to cut off supplies and food until the strikers paid their existing bills. Of course, strikers without income had no money to pay bills. Children and adults were going to bed hungry. Strikers faced daunting debt with little hope that the owners would negotiate in good faith.

Ana Clemenc was called to the county courthouse in Houghton to answer charges of assault and battery resulting from her arrest in August. A jury was named without a single immigrant member; instead it was comprised of only "Yankee" friends and colleagues of mine management. Clemenc was found guilty. Sentencing was delayed until January.

The Women's Alliance poured themselves into plans for the

Christmas party. These women knew firsthand just how discouraged their husbands were and how tenuous the strikers' resolve had become. They reserved the Italian Hall in the neighborhood of the Red Jacket mine and published notices of the party in the *Miners' Bulletin* and local foreign-language newspapers.

The Italian Hall was a relatively new building on Seventh Street in Calumet. It was a multiuse structure, with a saloon and grocery store on the ground floor and a large, "social" room, complete with a stage, theater seats, and an open area for dancing on the second floor.

On Christmas Eve, 1913, nearly two hundred children crowded the Italian Hall. Ana Clemenc, called "Annie" by the children and adults alike, directed the celebration. Lunch was followed by music and entertainment, including a young ballet dancer decked out in a pink ballet skirt and leotards. Most of the miners' children had never seen such a wonderful sight. A hired Santa Claus arrived. The children were delighted. One by one, the children marched across the small stage to receive a Christmas gift from "Saint Nick."

While Christmas music was played on the piano, the gift giving continued. Suddenly a loud man's voice shouted, "fire." Adults and children alike began to scream.

The children set up a wailing cry and headed for the narrow stairway to the first-floor exit. Although reports given afterward were inconsistent, records generally indicate that no fire existed. Some witnesses claimed the cry of "fire" came from a tall man in an overcoat with an upturned fur collar used to hide his face.

Ana and Mrs. Kaisor, the pianist, tried to calm the children. But as the shout of "fire" continued, the whole crowd rushed to the staircase. One striker, who had been placed in the doorway to ensure that only strikers' children entered the party, desperately tried to stop the flood of children. He was knocked to the floor and tumbled down the stairs, pushed by the force of the crowd.

At the bottom of the staircase, the door was shut. Whether it was locked from the outside or, for some reason, the frightened children couldn't open it, the result was that all access to the exit was blocked. In the room above, Ana and other adults frantically tried to stop the disaster. They failed.

Running children continued to fill the stairwell. Those closest to the door were pushed against it by the sheer weight of the pressing bodies and suffocated. Somehow, an emergency call reached the fire station, about a block away. The siren sounded and the fire chief ran by foot to the Italian Hall. He pulled open the stairway doors to find bodies of dead and dying children piled waist-high. The fire chief began pulling children from the crush.

By evening, seventy bodies were laid out in the hall amid the tables and Christmas decorations.

Ana Clemenc and some other witnesses claimed the man who cried fire wore a Citizens' Alliance button on his coat. Union leader Charles Moyer publicly called the incident "mass murder" and said he held mine owners responsible for every lost life.

Chaos gripped the whole community. In nearby Hancock, another mining town, the Finnish-language newspaper printed an emergency edition. Editors claimed that mine employees had blocked rescue efforts and Citizens' Alliance members had cheered. These charges were false. Still, they fanned the fires between strikers and miners. The editors were arrested and charged with sedition.

By Christmas morning news of the tragedy reached the whole nation. Donations poured in for strikers and their families. The C&H owners, aware of the power of public opinion, wrote a five-thousand-dollar check. Wealthy residents of Houghton, Hancock, and Calumet raised twenty-five thousand dollars.

The strikers called the donations "blood money" and refused them. When well-meaning neighbors and community members tried to visit striking families to offer their condolences, they were turned away. An outraged Ana Clemenc, according to reports, chased a visiting couple down the street.

At this point, Citizens' Alliance members tried to convince union leader Charles Moyer to accept the alliance money and use it for funeral costs. Moyer refused. The miners, Moyer said, would take care of their own.

Sheriff Cruse visited Moyer and demanded that he recant his charges that mine owners were responsible for the Italian Hall disaster. Again, Moyer refused. Soon after, a third group stormed into Moyer's hotel room. Moyer was shot and dragged from the hotel and across the Portage Lake Bridge. Some witnesses claimed the crowd shouted, "Hang him," and, "Throw him into the lake."

Whether those advocates of lynching or drowning were overruled or whether the claim is without merit, Moyer, still bleeding and injured, was forced onto a late-night train bound for Chicago.

A mass funeral was planned. Church services were held in Calumet's Catholic and Protestant churches. Afterward, mourners filed into the street and headed, en masse, toward the cemetery. The bodies of adults were carried by wagons to Lakeview Cemetery. The fathers and brothers carried children's caskets more than two miles to graves dug by the striking men. Some reports placed the number of mourners at more than fifty thousand people. A newsreel camera recorded the event.

Reports indicated that Ana Clemenc led the mourners while carrying the same silk American flag she had carried in the daily marches that began the strike. Days later, when interviewed by reporters, Clemenc said she was no longer certain that the man who had shouted fire had worn a Citizens' Alliance button.

In January Clemenc reported to the county jail to serve her ten-day sentence for assault and battery. After her incarceration she left Calumet.

Ella Reeve Bloor, a union organizer, socialist, and journalist, asked Clemenc to accompany her on a speaking and fund-raising tour of the Midwest. Bloor had worked to resolve strikes in other states. Eight years earlier, she had worked for six months in the Chicago stockyards to investigate working conditions. Upton Sinclair's famous book *The Jungle* was based on Bloor's experiences.

Bloor and Clemenc traveled the region by train, speaking about labor issues, raising consciousness in the citizenry, and raising funds for strikers and their families. They returned in March or early April with less money than they had at the beginning of the venture.

In the early weeks of 1914, the local union folded. The Western Federation of Miners followed. The strike was resolved, if such a term could accurately be used, by a congressional investigation that gave the miners an eight-hour workday and lower production requirements. However, the one-man "widow-maker" drill continued in use, and real wages didn't increase for mine workers.

Sometime between the escalation of the strike in early fall and Ana Clemenc's return to Calumet with Ella Bloor, she met and became attracted to a Slovenian newspaper editor from Chicago, Frank Shavs. Whether the Clemencs' marriage had deteriorated as a result of the strike or whether Ana was caught up in the romantic idea of life with a big-city journalist, history has not recorded.

In April 1914 she left Calumet and joined Shavs in Chicago. The couple married and had a daughter that year. The marriage was unsuccessful. Frank was an alcoholic, and Ana was sometimes forced to work two jobs to support the family. No evidence exists that she continued public union activism.

Ana Klobuchar Clemenc Shavs died in 1956 in Chicago. Twenty-four years later Michigan's governor declared June 17, 1980, "Ana Clemenc Day" in the state, honoring her as a leading figure in the history of copper mining and union activism in the Upper Peninsula.

MARGUERITE
LOFFT DE ANGELI

1889-1987

A Story to Tell and Vision to Tell It

"GOING BACK TO LAPEER WAS REALLY GOING HOME," Marguerite de Angeli wrote in her autobiography, *Butter at the Old Price.* And throughout her long life, she returned again and again to the small town where she spent most of her first thirteen years.

Marguerite's childhood could be described by the words of country singer Loretta Lynn, "We didn't know we were poor." The Lofft family moved from cottage to house to rental flat as finances permitted. Marguerite said her parents' love was a foundation in the midst of change.

Marguerite's beloved "papa," Shadrach George Lofft, was an artist, photographer, and family man. When business was good, and people wanted photographs, the Loffts rented a sprawling house with a yard for gardening. When times were "tight," Marguerite shared an attic bedroom with her sisters because the family had moved to a tiny, rented cottage.

Marguerite remembers her mother, Ruby Tuttle Lofft, as "not pretty, but lovely." "Mama" was firm but encouraging. While Papa

MARGUERITE LOFFT DE ANGELI

stoked the fires of creativity in his artistic eldest daughter, Mama passed on the discipline Marguerite would need to become a professional writer and illustrator. Mama had high expectations for her children. Compliments seemed too much like flattery to this firm but loving mother. But Mama did encourage the Lofft children—they were always told they could do anything they really wanted to do.

Lapeer was home for the Loffts; both Ruby and George's families lived in the small town in northern Michigan.

When Marguerite was a small child, the family relocated to Chicago, arriving just in time for the great Chicago World's Fair. The Loffts loved the fair exhibits. They didn't need money to enjoy the beauty and culture that had arrived at their front door.

Marguerite remembered turbaned men leading camels, miniature locomotives, and child-size houses with sod roofs and miniature furniture. She remembered Mama saying one exhibit was from far-away Japan, across the "great ocean."

In Chicago Marguerite discovered art and color. Her father had been commissioned to complete a portrait using "pastels," perhaps oil pastels or artist's chalk. Little Marguerite found the pastels, and an artist was born!

In her autobiography Marguerite wrote, "Nearby, on another barrel top, stood a portrait my father was doing . . . it was unfinished . . . I didn't touch the head, but I used every color in the box on the empty corner nearest me. . . . What excitement to feel the soft touch on the canvas, to see the bright mark it made. Pink, fiery red, orange, violet, cool blue, and green. What wonder! I could not stop until I had tried them all."

The Loffts stayed in Chicago less than two years before financial woes and longing for family drove them back to Lapeer. There, a large, extended family waited.

Grandpa Lofft had emigrated as a young man from England to Canada as an apprentice indentured to his grandfather. Indenture required seven years of work. In turn his grandfather would teach him the blacksmith's trade. At his grandfather's death he worked the remaining years of his contract for his grandmother.

A blacksmith, musician, storyteller, and pillar of the church choir, Marguerite's "grandpa" married his sweetheart, Maggie Sloan, in Ontario, Canada, in 1862. During their early marriage they moved to Lapeer, Michigan.

Michigan was growing. As many people said, "Lumber was king." Logging companies were clear-cutting the great forests of New York and the Midwest. In Michigan, a young blacksmith and his new wife could find cheap land and steady work.

The story of Marguerite Lofft's family touches the history of the United States at many points. Like many settlers and immigrants in the mid-1800s, Grandma and Grandpa Lofft came from western Europe. For them, America meant land and opportunity.

Marguerite traced her family tree back to England, Scotland, and Ireland. On her mother's branch of the tree, she discovered Puritan preacher Jonathan Edwards. A bit further out on that branch, she found famous Revolutionary War-era traitor Benedict Arnold!

The Tuttle family line also included Walter and Nancy Hough, pioneers who risked their lives bringing family and possessions from New York to Detroit by way of the Erie Canal and from Detroit to Almont by oxcart. They were true pioneers, building a log cabin with nothing but an axe and muscle. Nancy and Walter had six children. Nancy died in childbirth, and Walter married again. His second wife was mother to seven more children.

As an adult, Marguerite de Angeli wrote and illustrated twenty-nine of her own books and illustrated many more. These books were drawn from her life and the life of her family. Most were set in the history and places her family knew and on which they left their marks.

Mennonite and Quaker characters in Marguerite's book *Thee, Hannah* and Caldecott winner *Yonie Wondernose* reflect her years in Pennsylvania "Dutch" country. After living in urban Philadelphia, she wrote *Bright April,* the story of a black child in that city.

One of Marguerite's first books came straight from her family's long history in Lapeer, Michigan. *Copper-Toed Boots,* named one of Michigan's most notable books, was published in 1938. The "hero" was Shadrach—patterned, of course, after Marguerite's own father.

Most of Marguerite de Angeli's books depict a time and place in American history. She wrote character-driven stories, and her main character was almost always a child, like her readers. De Angeli's purpose wasn't to teach history but to introduce young readers to characters facing challenges.

Copper-Toed Boots is the story of a young boy growing up in Michigan in the 1870s. The boy's father is, of course, a blacksmith. Marguerite filled *Copper-Toed Boots* with family stories and tales from life in Lapeer. In the book Shadrach and his partner-in-crime "Ash" maneuver a calf up to the attic of the new school and tie its tail to the bell rope. The fictional Shadrach's grandma stitches ball fringe along the side seams of "grandpa's" Sunday trousers, just as Marguerite's own grandmother once did as a practical joke.

Copper-Toed Boots includes a circus parade down Nipsing Street, Lapeer's actual "main street." And, as the title indicates, Shadrach wanted copper-toed boots. But money was scarce, so he swept floors, picked berries, hauled water, ran errands, and finally saved a horse from drowning to earn store-bought, red leather boots with shiny, copper-covered toes.

Growing up surrounded by family in small-town Lapeer shaped Marguerite's character. During her entire life family was her center and primary focus. Lapeer also influenced her art and writing. De Angeli often drew stories from her life in Lapeer. One story about home-churned butter, small-town jealousy, and a houseful of busy toddlers provided the title for her autobiography. The story happened on Nipsing Street in "downtown" Lapeer, where Marguerite could walk to Uncle Ben Perkins's law office or Uncle Charlie's grocery. She could climb the steps to her own father's photography studio in rented rooms above a shop.

Across the street she could peek through the windows of her Uncle Denny's jewelry store. And, one block down, was Uncle Steve's General Store, where farm women traded butter and eggs for sugar, salt, and coffee. The best butter in town was always brought by Aunt Ella Tuttle—of the very-extended Tuttle clan, which still boasts descendants in the Lapeer area today. Aunt Ella's butter commanded the top price of sixteen cents per pound!

Prestige being a precious commodity for a small-town housewife,

Mrs. Desireau was jealous of Ella Tuttle's famous butter. So, she determined to beat her rival. Ella Tuttle wouldn't be the only butter maker in town earning sixteen cents per pound!

On a warm morning Mrs. Desireau had churned cream and was beating the butter with a wooden paddle when she noticed the fire needed "mending." She carefully placed the butter-filled bowl on the floor to tend the fire. No sooner was her back turned, then one of her children sat smack in the middle of the butter. "Oh well," she sighed. "It's butter at the old price, again."

This became a saying for the Loffts and, later, for the de Angeli family. Whenever something went wrong—a board sawed too short, a soggy pie crust, or a drawing that just didn't come together, they would say, "Oh well, it's butter at the old price again."

In Lapeer the Loffts' financial situation improved. When Papa got a job requiring frequent travel to New York, they rented a larger house. The new house had "modern plumbing" and space for gardens. But Marguerite missed Papa terribly. Supporting a family as a small-town photographer was, as Marguerite wrote later in her autobiography, "uphill work."

In the tiny Lapeer school, Marguerite excelled. In those early years of the twentieth century, every third grader memorized multiplication tables and every fourth grader recited the poem "Abou Ben Adhem." Marguerite discovered Shakespeare's *Romeo and Juliet* in fifth grade.

Marguerite's teachers often said, "You're daydreaming again." She was a daydreamer, a child who wanted to paint and write. She sketched around the edges of arithmetic assignments and added swirls to the pattern of the paper on her bedroom wall.

With Papa often gone, Marguerite's mother needed relief, so the children were shipped off to relatives during the summers. Marguerite visited Aunt Ella, maker of the now-famous butter. At Aunt Emma's, Uncle Denny would slip a secret quarter into her hand when she helped with dusting. One favorite summer memory was discovering Hawthorne's *Wonder Tales* and a book of Greek myths while visiting Uncle Ben.

At age eleven Marguerite visited her Uncle Will and his family in Detroit. As a treat they visited Wonderland. This was probably Detroit's then-famous "Wonderland Temple of Varieties," a performance hall showcasing everything from traveling theater troops to "curiosity" and animal shows. They saw curiosities exhibited in a series of rooms. In one Marguerite saw monkeys. In another, the entire room turned upside down when they entered. Marguerite was in awe. It was 1901, a new century. And, she'd seen monkeys and five automobiles!

When Marguerite was twelve years old, her father quit the job in New York. He was simply gone too often. The family moved into a small cottage, and George returned to the photography studio on Nipsing Street. Perhaps he could make a go of the business this time.

But, business didn't "go" anywhere. In spring of 1902 Eastman Kodak Company was hiring product demonstrators. Money and work were scarce in Lapeer, so Mama and Papa made another big decision. George would take the job, and the family would move to Philadelphia.

Papa left immediately. Mama shipped the children off to relatives and the household goods to Philadelphia. Marguerite's last weeks in Michigan were spent surrounded by family.

Marguerite was now age thirteen. This girl who had marveled to see five automobiles in a single week was about to move to a big city. The Lofft family left Lapeer by train for Buffalo, New York, and Philadelphia. Images from the trip and the wondrous city of Philadelphia appear in many of Marguerite's books.

The train journey was exhausting. They couldn't afford a sleeping car and ate food packed by their grandma back in Michigan. When they arrived in Philadelphia, Marguerite was enthralled. She heard the ringing of trolley bells and hucksters shouting, "Corn, buy your corn," or "Pretzels, one for a penny." Papa had rented a brick row house on Baring Street.

Philadelphia was an adventure. The family visited the Horticultural Hall and the historical museum. Marguerite discovered the public library. She sketched and dreamed. She heard John Philip Sousa's band and took singing lessons.

In the fall of 1904 Marguerite entered Girls' High School, studying French, German, Latin, English, mathematics, botany, drawing, music, and "gymnasium" in preparation for college.

For many years Marguerite was a paid member of church choirs. Her voice teacher once remarked, "You have a fine voice, though you'll probably turn out like your mother, and have six children." (She did!)

Once, the famous Oscar Hammerstein offered Marguerite a place in his choir—and an invitation to tour Europe. But her parents pointed out that traveling in Europe would take her away from Daily de Angeli, a musician who had been courting her with such enthusiasm that Papa said, "Tell that boy he doesn't have to leave something behind every time. He's welcome to come whenever he wants."

Marguerite married Daily de Angeli (and never toured Europe with Hammerstein). The newlyweds settled in Canada, where "Dai" put his background as a musician to work as a salesman for the Edison Phonograph Company. They lived in Toronto, Ontario, Winnipeg, and Saskatoon. Dai was a top salesman. The company sent him to open the new Minneapolis office. Their first baby, Jack, arrived.

Arthur was born and, about a year later, Ruby Catherine. Then World War I began. Dai found work in Philadelphia and they—all five of them—headed "home."

The following spring, Ruby Catherine died. The loss was crushing. Dai and Marguerite couldn't bear being in their house, where every sight sparked memories of Ruby Catherine. So they moved again. Marguerite found an art class in the neighborhood, and her long-neglected love of drawing became a balm for her grief.

Marguerite found her "artist's eye." She wrote in her autobiography, "The need to search for oneself led to many discoveries: rich color where one had never seen color . . . a style, an originality of one's own."

In 1918 the United States entered the war. Dai wanted to enlist, but Marguerite was pregnant again. Instead, he found "war work" at the Philadelphia Naval Base. This was a bitter time. Marguerite's sister Nina died. The flu epidemic of 1918 struck like a tidal wave, and the fourth de Angeli baby was born while Marguerite was hospitalized with fever.

Of course, the art classes ended and Marguerite packed her palette and brushes away.

Three years later, Maurice Bower, a professional illustrator, moved in across the street. Marguerite recorded the story of this friendship in her autobiography. Bower and Marguerite met, and although the man seemed doubtful that this thirty-year-old mother of three "had what it would take" to be serious about her art, he agreed to look at her work. However, she didn't have any work to show!

Dai ordered an easel, paper, and charcoal, and Marguerite set up "shop." She drew during the children's naps and between chores. She drew with toddlers clinging to her skirts. For one year she drew and drew and drew.

At the end of one year, Marguerite showed her work to two editors and received assignments from both.

Marguerite wrote in her autobiography, "From that day in 1922 . . . there has been an almost unbroken chain of illustration for Sunday school papers, magazines, and books. But it was fourteen years and two more children before I began writing my own books."

Marguerite's journey as a writer and illustrator was frustrated by detours. During the Depression, Dai and Marguerite lost their home.

Their sons couldn't attend college. Arthur went to Lapeer, where a cousin hired him to paint the city waterworks. Fortunately, painting the gingerbread trim on the Victorian-era building took all summer!

The Depression years strained Marguerite almost to the breaking point. They moved to rural Pennsylvania, hoping to "make do" with a kitchen garden and chickens. Dai's elderly mother and deaf sister became destitute and joined the family. Marguerite took every available illustration job for much-needed income. She contracted typhoid fever from tainted milk and had a complete physical and emotional collapse from which it took nearly two years to recover.

The de Angelis still depended on Marguerite's income from illustration. At the encouragement of an editor in New York, she decided to write and illustrate a children's book. Her own children appeared in this classic picture book, *Ted and Nina Go to the Grocery Store*. It was to be the first of many successful writer-illustrator projects for Marguerite de Angeli.

Like every good writer, de Angeli wrote about what she knew. She wrote about immigrants, shipwrecks, pirates, and children. One character was dubbed the "Pennsylvania Dutch Curious George." In five different books she created characters patterned after her German-Mennonite neighbors in Pennsylvania.

In 1949 a musician friend with a physical disability suggested she write about a child with a disability. The resulting book, *The Door in the Wall*, received the prestigious Newbery Award for Children's Literature. Robin, the hero of *The Door in the Wall*, learns, "it is better to have crooked legs than a crooked spirit." He shows real courage by using, not "overcoming," his disability.

De Angeli wrote *Bright April*, considered the first modern children's book about an African-American child. Long before the Civil Rights era, de Angeli wrote about racial prejudice.

Marguerite de Angeli's last years were filled with love and loss. At age eighty-eight she wrote and illustrated a book set in the early days of railroading. When she was ninety-four, a collection of her poems was published.

Her beloved Dai died just before their sixtieth wedding anniversary. Marguerite remained among the living, writing, painting, and loving her growing crowd of grandchildren, for eighteen more years.

Marguerite Lofft de Angeli has been honored again and again for her contributions to literature for children, both as an author and illustrator. She never forgot her family home of Lapeer, and the City Library was renamed in her honor in 1981. Three years later she was inducted into the Michigan Women's Hall of Fame.

Upon receiving the Newbery Medal in 1950 for *The Door in the Wall,* de Angeli remarked that she'd always told her children if you kept looking, no matter how long or high the wall, you will always find a door. She said, "Receiving the Newbery Medal has been for me a wonderful open door, which I hope will lead to more and better books."

In 1979, on her ninetieth birthday, Michigan's governor named March 14 "Marguerite de Angeli Day." Marguerite de Angeli continued to write and illustrate books until her death on June 16, 1987.

GWEN FROSTIC

1906–2004

Northland Artist

"FREEDOM IS A STATE OF MIND," Gwen Frostic often said. This artist, writer, philanthropist, and hard-edged businesswoman lived as though freedom was her undisputed birthright.

Obstacles to freedom for Gwen were numerous. A childhood illness, perhaps polio, left her with physical limitations. She never married. She started a business just before the Depression. Traditional women's careers in teaching or nursing didn't fit Gwen's temperament. Instead, her professional interests and entrepreneurial spirit left her isolated in the male-dominated world of business.

Still, Gwen was free. "I never found any obstacles," she told a reporter. "People cannot be discriminated against unless they allow themselves to feel that way."

Gwen's large family nurtured independence, creativity, and a near-Puritan work ethic. Fred Frostic was a gentle, literate teacher. He wrote books and articles and knew Latin names for plants. His love of woodworking, furniture making, music, and art presented a living example to his creative eldest daughter.

GWEN FROSTIC

Gwen's mother, Sarah, was a no-nonsense woman. Neighbors said she "wore the pants" in the Frostic household. One family story recounts a trip from Detroit by "steam engine." The train didn't stop in Wyandotte, where Sarah wanted to debark. Sarah refused to ride to the next station and hire a taxi. She insisted. And, in the end, the train stopped in Wyandotte.

After a serious illness in infancy, Gwen struggled to walk. Her motor-control skills and coordination were impaired. Her father said the family simply redefined walking.

"We called it walking," Fred Frostic said, "when she could go from one place . . . to the other on her feet, regardless of how many times she fell."

"When there are nine kids in a family, you have to be strong," Gwen once told a reporter. "Growing up in a big family trained me to think quickly. If you didn't, you missed your chance."

Born in 1906, Gwen was Sarah and Fred Frostic's second child. For four years the family lived in Croswell, a crossroads–general store–hitching-post sort of town. By the time the family moved to St. Charles, Michigan, in 1910, two more children, Helen and Ralph had been added to the family.

Gwen was pulled to first grade in a two-wheeled cart. Helen had been sent to school one year early to help her sister.

"What's the matter with your sister?" a neighbor child asked.

"Nothing," Helen would reply. "What's the matter with you?"

When Gwen was eleven years old, she and her family relocated to Ann Arbor, where Fred completed a bachelor's degree in education. At that time teachers commonly completed only a two-year "normal school" program. Fred wanted the challenge and financial security available to university graduates. He found both as superintendent of schools in the Detroit suburb of Wyandotte.

In Wyandotte the Frostic family had come home. They rented a sprawling frame house on Oak Street next door to the Mehlhose ice-cream factory. With his knowledge of botany and the children's labor, Fred created a Japanese-style garden, perennial beds, and terraced rock gardens of native ferns and wildflowers. The backyard became a miniature nature preserve. And, always, the Frostics kept a family dog.

Gwen inherited her father's love of nature. In her early career she created images of birds and wildlife from their Wyandotte yard. Later, when she purchased land in northern Michigan for her home and studio, she chose property surrounded by nature.

On that property Gwen designed and built a fieldstone, wood, and glass structure. Ducks and waterbirds winged down to the pond and wetlands just steps away. And, always, Gwen kept a dog.

In an era when children with disabilities attended "special" schools or stayed home, the Frostics never assumed Gwen couldn't or shouldn't do anything. After supper Gwen washed dishes. One brother dried. A second brother stood at the open pantry door. Dishes were tossed from person to person until they reached the pantry shelves—or "died" along the way. Sarah and Fred didn't notice, or perhaps didn't mind, the plate-tossing casualties.

The Frostic children were encouraged to explore. Sometimes Sarah would give them trolley fare to the town of Grosse Isle. The siblings roamed the woods and water all day. More than once, they spent their return fare on ice cream and walked home instead. Gwen made the eight-mile trek just like everyone else.

Once, Gwen and her brothers boiled the flesh from a dead rat so they could assemble the skeleton. Fred peeked into the kitchen, saw the rat, and walked away, telling Sarah they were just boiling water.

In high school Gwen was known as an artist and independent person. No girls had ever taken mechanical drawing. Gwen signed up. She was smart, talented, and held her own opinions. In the early 1920s many girls hid such qualities so boys would appear smarter and more talented and capable. Not Gwen.

Gwen was voted class artist. The Wi-Fi yearbook includes her in a "Senior Alphabet" with the words, "F is for Frostic, an artist named Gwen, who has talent for painting with brush and with pen." After graduation Gwen studied art education at Michigan State Normal College.

In 1926 Gwen transferred to Western Michigan University in Kalamazoo. The campus consisted of three imposing, columned buildings on a steep hill. Students climbed more than one hundred stairs or used a rachet-and-gear-style cable car. Gwen boarded in a rooming house near campus.

At Western Gwen carved her first linoleum block into the image of a monkey. She studied with Professor Lydia Siedschlag in the Fine Arts Department. Professor Siedschlag became a mentor and friend. Her influence on Gwen's development as an artist is evident in their friendship, which continued long after Gwen left Kalamazoo.

Biographers and friends suggest that other instructors saw art education as a realistic way for a "handicapped" woman to become self-supporting. Professor Siedschlag encouraged Gwen as an artist. Many years later, Gwen donated three stained-glass windows for Western's newly built Kanley Chapel. She dedicated one window to Lydia Siedschlag. The remaining two were dedicated to her father and herself.

In 1927 Gwen left Western Michigan without graduating. At that time her father was completing a master's degree at the University of Michigan. Her parents, who valued education so highly, were displeased. However, they supported Gwen's decision.

Gwen spent a single year teaching art. It's unknown whether her creative, independent temperament was poorly suited for teaching or whether students couldn't see the person behind Gwen's limping gait and slurred speech.

A shop was set up in the basement of the Oak Street house for Gwen. She purchased fifty to one hundred pounds of copper and brass in Detroit, hauled the materials to her workshop, and her business, Metalcraft, was born.

Gwen pounded and cut copper and brass into intricate metalwork. Her creations were part art, part practical. They included a delicately wrought fireplace screen depicting a dragon in flight and a copper sundial more than three feet high.

Metalcraft was barely on its feet when the stock market crashed. Gwen's brothers lost their jobs. Homeless men often knocked on Sarah's door, begging for supper.

During the Depression years, Gwen found creative ways to earn a living. She taught metal-crafting classes at the Detroit YMCA. Her sculpturelike creations in copper and brass were unusual and beautiful. Her reputation as an innovative artist spread until, one day, she received a custom order from Mrs. Henry Ford.

Gwen created two copper flower vases for Mrs. Ford. With typical bluntness Gwen later revealed they cost twenty-five dollars each. "I charged her what I charged everyone else," Gwen said.

During the Depression Gwen's siblings left home one by one for college or marriage. Gwen seemed challenged and happy to support herself creating art. As the Depression ended, her business grew. Then, in 1935, life changed dramatically.

Although Sarah Frostic had long suffered from high blood pressure, she refused to take prescribed medicine. On January 30, 1935, she was paralyzed by a massive stroke. Three days later, she died.

The Frostic family had never been emotionally expressive. However, Gwen wept when she told the news to the youngest Frostic, seven-year-old Margaret. The family grieved but rarely spoke about their loss. It fell to Gwen to become mother and homemaker. Neither role came naturally.

Gwen would work all day and then fix supper or wash clothes. She was as unorthodox as a fill-in mother as she'd been as a student and artist. Margaret remembered they once chose red linoleum for the kitchen. After it was installed, Gwen hated the results, so they painted over it.

In 1936 Fred Frostic remarried. His new wife, Florence, a former French teacher, took over the household. Gwen was thoroughly relieved. A biographer recorded that Florence was appalled at the condition of the house. After spending an hour cleaning, Florence hinted that Gwen could have done a better job of housekeeping. Gwen was unimpressed. "In an hour," she said, "I made $40 worth of stationery."

Freed from homemaking responsibilities, Gwen dove headlong back into her business. Although she joined community and social clubs and loved to visit Detroit, Gwen showed no interest in marriage.

"I wanted to be . . . free to work as long as I wanted and do what I wanted when I wanted to. . . . I'm not saying it's for everyone, but it's my way. I wanted to be free." And besides, as friends recalled her saying often, "I've always had a dog."

In 1941 the United States entered World War II. Bill Frostic enlisted as a physician in the Army Air Corps. Andy Frostic enlisted as a dentist.

With metal needed for military purposes, Gwen couldn't obtain copper and brass. Without consulting anyone, she closed Metalcraft and went to work at the Ford Motor Company's Willow Run bomber plant. Her family was shocked. But Gwen wanted to do her part for her country and her brothers.

At Willow Run nearly half the workers were women, and most worked on the assembly lines. Gwen put her artist's eye and metalworking experience to good use as a tool-and-die designer. For four years she worked six days a week from 8:00 in the morning until 5:30 at night.

Gwen found an apartment in Ann Arbor and commuted to work with women at Willow Run. She was "alone, but never lonely" because she started another business in her few spare hours.

Gwen was an entrepreneur at heart, so she began to think of ways to support herself as an artist. She found a secondhand electric printing press and a source of paper. She experimented with linoleum block carving and printing. From these experiments in art and enterprise, Presscraft Papers emerged.

On weekends Gwen carved linoleum blocks with images from nature and printed stationery and note cards. During the week she worked at Willow Run and filled orders for letterhead, advertising, and business cards in the evenings. She rented a small storefront in Wyandotte and opened her first retail shop.

At the end of the war, Gwen returned to Wyandotte and moved into the back room of her shop. She lived simply, funneling all receipts back into Presscraft Papers. She expanded to mail-order sales. Presscraft Papers took all of Gwen's time. And that was the way she liked it.

The death of her brother, William, was the single, dark moment during those years of busyness and creativity. Bill died in Hawaii in a plane crash. Gwen discovered she was beneficiary of his military life insurance policy. Perhaps Bill wanted to provide for Gwen in the event of his death. For the rest of her life, even as owner of a multi-million dollar business, Gwen received a monthly check for forty-two dollars. Those checks were a lifelong reminder of her loving, gentle brother.

For about ten years Gwen's business in Wyandotte grew. As it did, Gwen became increasingly unhappy and restless. Bread-and-butter commercial printing had taken over the business, and the art printing Gwen loved was afforded less and less time. Something had to change.

With Gwen's encouragement and money, Fred Frostic built a summer cottage in Frankfort, in Michigan's "north woods." Here she rediscovered her love of nature. She walked the Lake Michigan shore, renewing her love of birds, flowers, and wild things.

Gwen spoke of closing shop to spend summers in Frankfort. Her siblings laughed. Then Fred Frostic died. One day, without consulting anyone, Gwen loaded everything she owned into a truck and moved "up north."

Gwen was part philosopher, part artist, and part shrewd business owner. "Dreams without work are fantasy," she said. "Work without dreams is drudgery."

As a single, self-employed woman, Gwen Frostic was unique in Frankfort. The tourist town was busy in summer and north-woods quiet all winter. This pace gave Gwen time to sit in the woods and sketch. She had time to carve new blocks and experiment with inks and colors. Gwen established an approach to business that changed little during the next forty years.

Gwen relied on word-of-mouth advertising. She created products summer tourists and women especially liked. At first, she did everything from design to carving blocks, to printing, packing, shipping, and bookkeeping. She kept costs down by mixing inks and declining "frills" such as packaging or fancy displays.

Gwen went out and found business. When the famous pianist Van Cliburn performed at nearby Interlochen Arts Center, Gwen printed the programs. In a restaurant she'd whip a few Presscraft napkins printed with her trademark nature images from her purse and suggest that the owners might prefer her beautiful products to place mats advertising the local fruit growers' co-op!

Presscraft Papers grew. Gwen added to the Frankfort shop. Her nephew, Bill, joined the business. One year Gwen filed federal income taxes listing her occupation as "printer." The IRS refused to believe a printer could make so much money! Gwen was and did.

In the 1960s Gwen moved to nearby Benzonia. Friends asked why anyone would move a successful business from the main street of a tourist town to a wooded wetland in the middle of nowhere. Gwen did it for herself.

"When I first went to buy this land," Gwen said of the 285-acre, wooded parcel, "it was ideal for an artist so I persisted.

[The owner] backed out of the deal three times because she started thinking there must be a pot of gold under some tree. I told her she should stop looking."

Gwen designed and supervised the building of Gwen Frostic Studios. Today, the wood, glass, and stone structure still houses the printing operation, the shop, and Gwen's home. Boulders from her beloved Michigan countryside form the exterior. She chose an old-fashioned sod roof. Bark-covered logs formed walls. Driftwood was transformed into shelves and hardware. When the floor was poured, Gwen directed workmen to press leaves, ferns, and animals' feet into the wet cement. When the shop opened, she'd tell children that bunnies, deer, and frogs had left their footprints at night!

April 26, 1964, on Gwen's fifty-eighth birthday, Gwen Frostic Studios opened in Benzonia with four Heidelberg presses and more than one thousand guests. Later, Gwen joked that they didn't have enough cookies!

In 1957 Gwen wrote and published *My Michigan,* the first of nineteen publications of her unique prints and prose. Some books were published in Braille.

Gwen spent many hours watching and sketching. She built four tiny "huts" on her property. To visitors these looked like the offspring of a duck blind and a screened porch. She wired one hut with electricity so she could brew coffee.

Gwen's block carvings became more subtle and complex. She experimented with new papers, images, and colors and applied production-line techniques learned at Willow Run to her printing operations. By the mid-1980s Gwen operated fifteen presses, and her shop was a tourist destination. Yet she continued to work every day and considered lunch with a friend or a Coke and Oreo cookies a treat.

Gwen had no patience with flattery, laziness, or complaining. She loved children. Friends recall she would "stock" the fieldstone fountain in her shop with pennies so "the children would have something to count."

People sometimes said Gwen's prices were too low or her designs too simple. Gwen never knew nor cared what competitors charged. Her books reflected her own philosophies and concerns.

Men in Frankfort's business community had avoided or openly disliked her. In Benzonia she was accepted by the business community and made friends among the women. She was active in the P.E.O. Sisterhood, a philanthropic organization dedicated to supporting education for women.

As Gwen's reputation grew, she received invitations to speak about business, nature, and the abilities and accomplishments of women. Although Gwen never learned to drive, she always owned a car. She'd draft a friend or her nephew Bill as driver.

In her biography of Gwen Frostic, author Sheryl James called the 1970s and 1980s Gwen's "golden age." Her business expanded. She was able to give, usually anonymously, to charities she valued. Her alma mater recognized her with an honorary Doctorate of Fine Arts. Other honors followed. In 1978 the governor designated May 23 as "Gwen Frostic Day" in Michigan. She received the Michigan Women's Hall of Fame Life Achievement award.

Gwen was honored so many times that she finally said, "I need another award like I need another case of shingles."

Gwen's work was her life. She reached eighty years of age. Then eighty-five. Then ninety. She continued to sketch and carve and write. Asked by a reporter if she was still creating, Gwen responded, "Am I still alive?"

In later years, she sometimes said that after her death, her shop and home should be left until nature reclaimed the land.

Gwen's death on April 25, 2001, came one day before her ninety-fifth birthday. Her will included clear instructions for her property and business. She'd established a very substantial endowment to Western Michigan University for art scholarships. Her beloved shop would continue under the ownership of friends Pam and Kirk Lorenz.

As always, Gwen spoke for herself: "I live as I believe and believe in the way I live. There never was a five-year plan. Each day, do the very best you can. . . . I've never said 'I wish I had.' "

ROSA PARKS

1913-2005

Sitting, Walking, and Standing for Civil Rights

AMERICANS HAVE HEARD THE STORY OF ROSA PARKS, a poor, black seamstress, exhausted after a long day, who did what no one had done before. She refused to give her seat on a Montgomery, Alabama, bus to a white man. People have heard how Rosa Parks sparked a bus boycott that, in turn, sparked the civil rights movement in America.

Many Americans know this version of Rosa Parks's story. However, this version isn't what actually happened.

Rosa Parks was a hero among heroes. But she wasn't an impoverished woman too tired to move. She wasn't a simple worker, caught up in Martin Luther King Jr.'s dream. She was actually a visionary who shared the dream of equality and opportunity for her people. She wasn't swept into the civil rights movement; she jumped.

On December 1, 1955, in Montgomery, Alabama, Rosa Parks did refuse to give her seat on a public bus to a white man. She described this moment in her autobiography, *My Story*, "[The bus driver] said, 'let me have those front seats. . . . Ya'll better make it light on yourselves and let me have those seats.'"

ROSA PARKS

Other black passengers moved. Rosa refused. She wrote in her autobiography that she could not see how standing up would "make it light" for her or anyone else.

"The more we gave in and complied, the worse they treated us," she wrote in *Quiet Strength*. "People always say that I didn't give up my seat because I was tired, but that isn't true. I was not tired physically. . . . No, the only tired I was, was tired of giving in."

The bus driver threatened to have Rosa arrested.

"You may do that," Parks responded. Within a short time the police arrived and Rosa Parks was taken to jail. She was finger-printed and locked in a cell. And, because officers refused to allow her the phone call that is every prisoner's legal right, hours passed before the news reached her family. Until then she was alone.

Born February 4, 1913, Rosa Louise McCauley was the daughter of Leona Edwards McCauley, a teacher, and James McCauley, a builder. Their hometown of Pine Level, Alabama, had changed little in the fifty years since slavery ended. Rosa's grandparents, Rose and Sylvester Edwards, had been enslaved as children. In their family stories of the long fight for equality were told from personal experience.

Because of his coloring, people sometimes thought Sylvester was white. He would often extend his hand to white men saying, "Edwards is my name." At that time, white men wouldn't shake a black man's hand. White people used black people's first names. But blacks were supposed to call whites "Miss" or "Mister."

Rosa's grandfather refused to accept such treatment. As a boy, he had defied a white overseer and been brutally beaten. As an adult, he was still defiant. Rosa watched and learned.

Rosa knew racism firsthand. Each day, from first grade through fifth grade, she passed the brick "white" school with its glass windows on her way to the one-room "colored" school. Although tax dollars from both black and white workers paid for the white students' building, the black community had to pay for and build its own.

It was called separate but equal. It was only separate.

During Rosa's childhood, the Ku Klux Klan was active in Pine Level. She remembered her grandfather sitting before the door of their house, his double-barreled shotgun in his lap. The Ku Klux Klan rode that night and many nights. Rosa slept in her clothes, ready to run.

Her grandfather vowed, "I don't know how long I would last if they came breaking in here, but I'm getting the first one who comes through the door."

Sylvester, Rose, and "Mama Leona" protected Rosa from seeing violence. But she heard about it anyway. She heard about beatings and rapes. She heard of lynchings.

Rosa's family was poor, but not desperately so. They raised chickens and a few cows. They grew vegetables, fruit, pecans, and walnuts. Leona received a small salary teaching in a "colored" school.

From the time she was age six or seven until Rosa left to attend high school in Montgomery, she and her family picked cotton. They earned fifty cents a day for chopping and one dollar per hundred pounds of picked cotton.

Until she was eight years old, Rosa rarely left Pine Level. A public bus covered the route between nearby Tuskegee and big-city Montgomery, but blacks weren't allowed to board. Black passengers rode with luggage on top of the bus.

So Rosa's first trip to Montgomery was by car. Mr. Barefoot, a Pine Level entrepreneur, provided taxi service for black passengers.

In Montgomery Rosa and her mother stayed with relatives. Blacks were unwelcome in hotels and most boardinghouses.

Leona's long-term plan was for Rosa to attend high school in Montgomery. There were no public high schools for black students in the area. Leona made enormous sacrifices to send her daughter to a private high school.

At age eleven Rosa boarded with relatives while attending Montgomery Industrial School or, as everyone black called it, "Miss

White's School." Alice White, a white woman from Massachusetts, founded the school to provide education and training for black girls. The faculty members were white Northerners. All the students were black.

In Montgomery Rosa had her first taste of institutionalized racism. Back in Pine Level racism was "just the way things were." In Montgomery racism was codified, approved, and written into law.

Public facilities, such as busses, drinking fountains, restrooms, and waiting rooms, were either segregated or closed to blacks altogether. Eleven-year-old Rosa wondered whether water in the "White" fountains tasted the same as water in the "Colored" fountains.

Rosa attended the Alabama State Teachers College for Negroes. At the beginning of eleventh grade, her grandmother became ill. At age sixteen she dropped out of school and cared for Grandma Rose until her death. Then Rosa returned to Montgomery and worked in a shirt factory. She tried to return to school, but her mother became ill. Once again, school was delayed while Rosa took care of a sick loved one.

Rosa met Raymond Parks, a bright young barber and civil rights activist. He drove from Montgomery to Pine Level to court her in a sporty red Nash with a rumble seat. Raymond, or "Parks" as everyone, including Rosa, called him, was Alabama-born and a longtime member of the NAACP, the National Association for the Advancement of Colored People.

When Rosa met Raymond Parks in 1931, Parks was raising defense funds and public awareness for the Scottsboro Boys, nine black men arrested and charged with raping two white women. The young men had been "hoboing" on a freight train, looking for work.

Although the women's testimony was inconsistent, no witnesses were found, and there was no evidence of a crime, let alone of guilt, the men were found guilty, and all but the youngest, a fourteen-year-old boy, were sentenced to death.

Raymond made their cause his cause. That was one of the qualities that attracted Rosa to him. Raymond Parks and others risked their lives to meet secretly in Montgomery. Police killed two organizers. Officers watched Rosa and Raymond's home. More than once, he had to sneak in the back door after a late-night meeting. Rosa supported the work of her husband-to-be, but she felt terrified for him as well.

Parks's group and others publicized the Scottsboro Boys' case. The U.S. Supreme Court ordered new trials for all defendants on the grounds that they had no credible representation at their first trials. Appeals dragged on for years. The last defendant was paroled in 1950.

In December 1932 Rosa and Raymond Parks married at her mother's house in Pine Level. They moved to Montgomery, where Parks was employed as a barber. Rosa returned to and graduated from high school, an uncommon accomplishment.

Rosa was hired at Maxwell Field, a nearby military base. Although at this time segregation and institutionalized racism were practiced by all branches of the U.S. military, public facilities on military bases were integrated by order of President Roosevelt. Thus began a strange time in which Rosa worked in an integrated environment every day and returned to segregated Montgomery every night. She rode to the base on a segregated bus, sitting in the back. Then, on base, she chose any seat on the integrated trolley and ate lunch in an integrated cafeteria.

When the Supreme Court ruling set aside the Scottsboro Boys' death sentences, Raymond and Rosa got involved in voter registration. In 1940 thirty-one black people were registered to vote in Montgomery. Black leaders formed the Voter's League, which met in the Parks's home.

In 1940 every U.S. citizen had the right to vote. But no federal law defined how voter registration should be done. Southern states kept black people from voting by making it difficult or impossible to register. First, southern states allowed only property owners to register to vote. Then, so-called "literacy" tests were used. Registration offices were open a few hours during the day, when most black people worked. Of course this served to keep black citizens from exercising their voting power.

The first time Rosa tried to register to vote she was told she failed the literacy test. She had no way to know whether this was true. Rosa took the test three times before she passed. But she still couldn't vote until she paid her "accumulated poll tax." This "tax" was $1.50 a year—for every year a person was eligible to vote. White voters registered at age twenty-one and paid the tax each year. Black voters were required to pay this tax retroactively. Since Rosa was kept from registering until she was thirty-two years old, she had to pay $16.40 in retroactive poll taxes. This policy prevented poor people from voting.

In the mid-1940s many black soldiers, including Rosa's brother Sylvester, returned from World War II. After fighting as equals on the battlefield, these men were unwilling to return to racism and Jim Crow segregation. A violent conflict was in the making.

Rosa Parks's first run-in with Montgomery's policy for public buses occurred one chilly winter afternoon in 1943. The bus was full. Black passengers crowded the aisles and blocked the back door, in spite of empty seats in the "white" section at the front. Rosa used the front door. The driver demanded she get off and board at the back. When she protested that the back doorway was blocked by standing passengers, the driver forced her from the bus. Like all Montgomery bus drivers, he was armed.

Rosa joined the NAACP. In the early 1940s she and a friend from Miss White's school were the only women members in Montgomery. Rosa became secretary. One of her jobs was to gather and disseminate information about unjust arrest, conviction, and incarceration of blacks.

Racial conflict increased. In 1949 the NAACP Youth Branch attempted to integrate the Montgomery Public Library. Repeatedly, they attempted to check out books at the main library instead of the poorly staffed and resourced "colored" library. Time and again they were refused.

The battle for civil rights seemed unending. Black teachers fought for equal pay. The NAACP took public school systems to court for denying equal education to black students.

During the summer of 1955, Rosa attended a workshop on school desegregation at the progressive Highlander Folk School in Tennessee. For the first time in her life, Rosa lived with white people. She wrote in her autobiography that she enjoyed the smell of morning coffee and, even more, enjoyed the knowledge that white people were making it for her instead of the other way around.

The Highlander School changed Rosa's image of racial relationships. For the first time she was able to forget skin color and simply relate to others as human beings. At summer's end, she returned to Montgomery—and the all-too-real world of racism and segregation.

In 1955 the NAACP considered legal challenges to segregation on public buses. Leaders had been talking about a bus boycott for some time. That spring, a teenager named Claudette Colvin was arrested for refusing to give up her seat on a bus. Black activists brought a petition to city officials asking for "better seating arrangements." As yet, no one dared to use the word *integration*. Still, they were refused.

Plans to bring the matter to court were shelved when it was learned that Colvin was pregnant. The NAACP knew their test case must be above reproach.

That summer, another arrest occurred. Then, in December, Rosa Parks's was the third arrest.

The NAACP defense committee considered Rosa the perfect

defendant. She would be convicted, they knew, of violating the segregation laws. Then, their plan was to appeal her case in a higher court. They weren't only seeking equal treatment on public buses, they wanted to change segregation law.

Black leaders decided it was time to stop requesting and begin demanding. During the second week of December 1955, they formed the Montgomery Improvement Association (MIA) and demanded courteous treatment, first-come, first-served seating (with blacks still sitting in the back), and hiring of black drivers. Until these demands were met, the black community of Montgomery vowed to boycott city buses.

White people in power believed any concession to these demands would open the door to integration. No one knew how long the boycott would last. Black citizens had no guarantee that changes would ever be made.

During the weeks that followed, the black community organized. Churches began volunteer-staffed shuttle services. Taxi drivers took black customers to and from work for just ten cents until the city arrested them for not charging full fare. And, each and every day, people walked.

When forbidden by his employers even to speak his wife's name, Raymond Parks quit his job. Rosa was "let go" from her job as a tailor. She became the full-time, unpaid transportation coordinator for the MIA. Each day about thirty thousand people were transported to and from work.

Buses became the front line of the battle for equality in Montgomery. While the black community organized, the Ku Klux Klan grew. Black leaders were threatened. The former NAACP president's home was bombed. Rosa Parks received death threats.

Meanwhile, Rosa Parks's lawyer, Fred Gray, filed a federal lawsuit challenging segregation laws. Rosa's conviction would be the test case.

The boycott continued. Mid-February, an old law prohibiting boycotts was unearthed. Eighty-nine blacks, including Martin Luther King Jr. and Rosa Parks, were arrested. A photo of Rosa's arrest appeared in the *New York Times* newspaper.

Martin Luther King Jr. was convicted of organizing an illegal boycott. Rosa Parks began speaking at civil rights fund-raisers in other states.

In June the MIA won its lawsuit. Segregation on public buses was ruled unconstitutional. The city appealed. The boycott dragged on. In November 1956 the Supreme Court upheld the ruling. But, even then, the boycott continued until December 21, 1956, when the official order was received and instituted.

The Montgomery bus boycott lasted 381 days. The problems weren't over.

Snipers fired at integrated buses. The homes and churches of black citizens were torched and bombed. Other bus boycotts began in Birmingham and Tallahassee, Florida. As Rosa Parks wrote in her autobiography, "the direct-action civil rights movement had begun."

In 1957 Montgomery became so dangerous for them that Raymond, Rosa, and Rosa's mother moved to Detroit. Raymond became licensed as a barber. Rosa worked as a seamstress when she wasn't speaking at civil rights conferences or demonstrations.

In Detroit Parks and Rosa remained active in civil rights work. Each year the movement gained momentum. Martin Luther King Jr. became a national leader.

Change came at great cost as white racists defended their power with violence. Children were killed in a Birmingham, Alabama, church bombing. Men were lynched. Peaceful marchers were beaten and arrested. But the movement would not be stopped.

In 1965 the Southern Christian Leadership Conference, a defining force in the civil rights movement, organized a march from

Selma to Montgomery, Alabama. Rosa Parks traveled from Detroit to participate.

After the march Viola Liuzzo, a white homemaker from Detroit, was shot by Klansmen while driving marchers back to Selma.

In 1965 Rosa was hired as an aide for John Conyers, the newly elected African-American congressman from Michigan. Then and for the next twenty-three years, Rosa kept Conyers's office running and helped needy constituents.

The fight for equality continued. Malcolm X was assassinated. Martin Luther King Jr. was shot and killed in Memphis. Senator Robert Kennedy was next. Black and white Americans grieved.

These deaths, coupled with years of violence, discrimination, and poverty, broke the black community's nonviolent resolve. Riots erupted in many cities. In 1967, forty-three people died and nearly two thousand were injured in the Detroit riots. Property damage was in the millions of dollars.

Still the Parks family remained in Detroit. Rosa had deep roots at St. Matthew's, a small African Methodist Episcopal congregation.

Between 1975 and 1980 Rosa's brother and mother died. Her beloved Raymond died of cancer in 1977. Her focus was drawn from community work and civil rights to caring for her family.

In 1987 Rosa Parks founded the Rosa and Raymond Parks Institute for Self-Development in Detroit. She retired from Representative Conyers's office to devote herself to institute projects and funding.

The institute offers scholarships, education, and community programs to youth in Detroit. One program, "Paths to Freedom," enables young people to actually trace the path of the Underground Railroad, visiting sites where history was made.

Rosa Parks was honored for her life's work. In 1996 she received the Presidential Medal of Freedom. In 1980 she received the Martin Luther King Jr. Nonviolent Peace Price. In Montgomery, Alabama, the bus route has been renamed Rosa Parks Boulevard.

Before her death on October 25, 2005, at age ninety-two, Rosa Parks wrote in *Quiet Strength,* "Laws against segregation have been passed and all that progress has been made. But, a whole lot of white people's hearts have not been changed."

She also wrote, "We still have a long way to go . . . it is better to continue to try to teach or live equality . . . than to have hatred or prejudice."

NANCY HARKNESS LOVE

1914-1977

Calling the Yankee Doodle Gals

"A PENNY A POUND, AND UP YOU GO," was the pitch to new customers from a pair of "barnstormers"—pilots who crisscrossed the countryside making money by performing stunts and taking eager small-town residents into the skies.

In the rural, northern Michigan town of Houghton, Nancy Harkness paid her weight in pennies to fly in the barnstormers' plane. She returned determined to fly herself.

The barnstormers didn't introduce Nancy to flying. When she was thirteen, she and her family were among the awestruck witnesses to Charles Lindbergh's landing in France after his solo crossing of the Atlantic Ocean.

Family tradition holds that Nancy announced, "I'm going to quit school and become a pilot, Daddy." Nancy's father agreed to let her take flying lessons—without, of course, the "quitting school" portion of her proposal. And, when her sixteenth birthday came, Nancy found an instructor and took off—quite literally.

Eighteen-year-old Jimmy Hanson gave lessons in an elderly Fleet plane. Nancy had to complete the instruction and log enough

NANCY HARKNESS LOVE

hours to earn her license. And, it all had to be accomplished before she left boarding school in less than three weeks.

Nancy once told a reporter, "I don't think he knew what made the plane stay in the air. At least, he never told me. My instructions were just to 'keep up the flying speed.'"

Nancy logged four and a half hours of flying between August 26 and August 30, 1930. The next day, August 31, she flew solo. In the following ten days, she logged ten hours in the air.

Jimmy Hanson must have taught his young student the basics, because on November 7, 1930, at age sixteen and a half, Nancy received her private pilot's license in the mail. She was in Massachusetts, in school at Milton Academy, a private boarding school for girls.

No one at Milton knew Nancy could fly. She used this to her advantage. With the ink barely dry on her pilot's license, Nancy and two friends rented a plane in Boston and headed to Poughkeepsie, New York. Nancy was inexperienced. When the weather limited visibility, she couldn't read her compass. Some gauges malfunctioned. Finally, she landed the plane. No one was hurt, but later Nancy called the landing "precarious." In truth it was a potentially fatal result of inexperience.

Back at school Nancy rented a plane at the local airport one weekend and "buzzed" the nearby boys school. Nancy's own daughter told biographer Sarah Rickman, "My mother still hadn't learned much about physics. . . . She nearly hit the bell tower and rattled some slates loose so they fell off the roof."

At first the Milton Academy faculty blamed the "Fuller boys," two local brothers with a reputation for pranks. But a quick phone call to the airport manager revealed the pilot was a female student named Miss Nancy Harkness. Nancy returned to school to find half the administration waiting in the residence hall for her.

In September 1931 Nancy enrolled at Vassar College in New York. By then her priorities were firmly established. Flying first and school second. She logged enough hours and instruction to obtain a limited commercial license by the end of her freshman year. In fact a national newspaper featured her as the "Flying Freshman."

Nancy began flying at a time when women were just entering the field. In January 1929 national records show thirty-one licensed women pilots in the United States. Just two years later, that number was three hundred. Amelia Earhart and other women made news in airplane races and distance-flight competitions. Although their participation was generally viewed as an amusing curiosity, the women took flying and their skill as pilots quite seriously.

In 1934 Nancy Harkness left Vassar. Financial downturns resulting from the stock market crash and the Depression made it impossible for her to continue college. She headed to Boston to put her training as a pilot to good use.

Although Nancy had earned both private and commercial licenses, she was unable to find employment as a pilot. She did find a flying-related job as a salesperson for Inter-City Air Service, a start-up company owned by Robert Love. In those money-tight Depression years, Inter-City offered every flight-related service imaginable. They provided passenger service, shuttle flights from East Boston Airport (now Logan International), instruction, and even aerial surveying.

During the next year Nancy and her boss, Robert Love, began a romantic relationship, albeit one interrupted by their dual careers. Nancy left Inter-City to work for the federal government's National Advisory Committee for Aeronautics (NACA). The agency, which eventually became known as the National Aeronautics and Space Administration, or NASA, set standards and maintained safe conditions for the fledgling industry.

Nancy was hired by the national Airport Marking and Mapping project to convince towns in the eastern United States to allow NACA to paint the town's name on the roof of a tall building or other landmark. Considering that planes had no radios, some airports were little more than cow pastures, and pilots often set out equipped with a paper road map or handwritten directions, even this small mapping effort was of value.

After two years with NACA, Nancy and Robert Love married in Nancy's hometown of Houghton, Michigan. Houghton residents thought the wedding of the pilot-daughter of the town doctor and his social-leader wife was romantic. They were amazed by the couple's honeymoon plans. Bob and Nancy were California bound, in an airborne version of a classic American road trip. Newspapers called her the "Flying Bride."

A few years later, war broke out in Europe, and, although the United States remained neutral, Bob Love joined the Army Air Corps as a Reserve pilot.

The British Royal Air Force (RAF) needed planes. Inter-City sold them. However, international law didn't allow airplanes from neutral nations to fly to any nation involved in the war.

How could Inter-City deliver planes to the RAF? One such delivery was handled—adhering to the letter, if not the spirit of the law—by Nancy. She landed a Stinson 105 plane in Maine, near the Canadian border. Then, the plane was pushed onto Canadian soil, and Nancy climbed back into the cockpit and flew to Halifax, Nova Scotia. From there the plane was shipped to England.

This unusual delivery gave Nancy an idea. Through Robert, she knew the Army Air Corps needed pilots to transport aircraft. Through her membership in the Ninety-Nines, an international organization for women pilots, she knew female pilots who would leap at the opportunity to fly professionally. In May 1941 Nancy drafted a letter to Col. Robert Olds proposing that women could ferry airplanes, thereby freeing men pilots for military flying.

Nothing came of Nancy's idea until 1942, after the bombing of Pearl Harbor catapulted the United States into World War II. The nation and the military were unprepared for war. Factories began day-and-night manufacture of military weaponry, equipment, and vehicles, including airplanes. Pilots were suddenly in great demand and short supply.

Fresh from the assembly line, airplanes had to be transported all over the country. But qualified male pilots were being hurried through combat training. By June 1942 the Air Transport Command (ATC), responsible for transporting airplanes, had only 384 pilots serving the entire U.S. Army. The ATC commander, Col. William Tunner, searched desperately for experienced pilots.

Meanwhile, Robert Love entered into the Army Air Corps full-time. He and Nancy moved to Washington, D.C., where Nancy worked for ATC's Ferrying Command in Baltimore. Here, a quirk of wartime rationing brought Nancy—and her idea—to the attention of the ATC.

To save time and because gasoline was more readily available for airplanes than for personal vehicles, Nancy commuted from Washington to Baltimore each day in their Fairchild 24 airplane. Of course her unusual transport became the topic of office gossip, and word reached Colonel Tunner.

As luck would have it, Tunner's office was near Robert Love's. Tunner asked Robert if the rumors of his "flying wife" were true.

"I'm combing the woods for pilots and here's one right under my nose. Are there many more women like your wife?" Tunner asked.

Bob Love suggested Tunner speak with Nancy directly. The resulting conversation set in motion an idea that would change the role of women as pilots in the military.

Nancy Love and Colonel Tunner met, and by June a plan was devised to create a plane delivery operation staffed by women pilots. Although army brass assumed women couldn't endure the physical demands of ferrying airplanes, desperate need forced the door open for a "small, controlled experiment."

The army christened the women pilots the Women's Auxiliary Ferrying Squadron. Of course, they were soon called the "WAFS."

Eighty-three telegrams were sent to members of the Ninety-Nine—barnstormers, flight instructors, and flying friends of Nancy's from around the country. Twenty-eight replies were received. Some applicants were college graduates. Others had paid for flight training by waiting tables. Many were certified flight instructors. Some were married and mothers. One woman had witnessed the arrival of Japanese bombers at Pearl Harbor. Another, a barnstormer, had logged more than three thousand hours of flight time.

Male military leaders limited the role of the WAFS at every point. For men employment with the ATC Ferrying Division required two hundred hours of flight experience. The WAFS were required to have five hundred hours. Men's salaries were three hundred dollars per month. The army provided housing and uniforms. Male pilots routinely "hitched" rides to or from ferrying assignments on military planes.

WAFS were paid $250 per month, with no military benefits. No provision was made for housing or uniforms. And, because some military brass thought any woman "hitching a ride" on a military plane would be perceived as a prostitute, WAFS had to travel to or from ferrying assignments by train or haul their B-4 flight bag and parachute to the nearest airport to wait for a commercial flight!

But, Nancy's recruits weren't concerned about limits. They wanted to serve their country, help the war effort, and fly! Barbara Erickson London, one of the youngest WAFS wrote in a letter, "I'd have flown those planes for free."

Because all WAFS recruits were experienced pilots, training began immediately. The army gave Nancy Love's pilots three months to prove themselves. The WAFS were publicly announced on September 10, 1942. Their squadron's first mission was in late October.

Ferries began with Piper Cubs, the army's smallest airplane. Those deliveries were completed without incident and on time. WAFS began to ferry larger and more powerful planes.

Although the WAFS base and Nancy Love's command remained at New Castle Army Air Base in Wilmington, Delaware, within months, WAFS were stationed near aircraft factories in California, Dallas, and Romulus, Michigan. Soon a WAFS pilot was flying somewhere in the United States nearly every hour of every day.

While her pilots were proving themselves, Nancy Love set out to expand the limits set by army officers who assumed women couldn't fly large planes. In early 1943 she learned to fly the P-51 Mustang, a "pursuit fighter" designed for air battles. One by one, Nancy and other WAFS pilots "tested out" by qualifying to fly some of the military's most powerful planes.

By spring WAFS pilots had such an outstanding record that the army lifted all restrictions, announcing that any ATC pilot could fly any plane on which that pilot had "tested out."

While Nancy Love was pouring herself into the WAFS, another woman pilot, Jackie Cochran, was pitching her own vision to the U.S. Army. Cochran had trained twenty-five American women pilots in England, where women pilots were already supporting the RAF by flying noncombat missions.

On September 10, 1942, Jackie Cochran returned to the United States. Plans were set for her to meet with Gen. Henry Arnold, head of flying for the U.S. Army. General Arnold had agreed to use women for noncombat flying.

That same day the army announced Nancy Love and the WAFS. With journalistic bias typical of the period, WAFS were portrayed in the media as glamorous "girls." Nancy Love was toasted as the most glamorous of all. Jackie Cochran couldn't know how horrified Nancy was by the publicity. She didn't know the army, not Nancy or the WAFS, was responsible for the utter absence of communication. Jackie Cochran was astonished and furious.

Jackie Cochran and General Arnold met. An agreement was reached continuing the much needed WAFS and authorizing Jackie to start the Women's Flying Training Detachment (WFTD), recruiting and preparing women pilots to fly military planes.

Unfortunately, the army's poor communication created a rift between Nancy and Jackie and the women they led. In fact the relationship between the two leaders was never mended. By the summer of 1943, WAFS were ferrying planes all over the nation and WFTD was training hundreds of women, both experienced pilots and novices. The army decided to combine the two programs, forming the Women's Air Service Pilots, or WASP.

Jackie Cochran was in command of the WASP. Nancy Love was named director of all ferrying operations. Formation of the WASP required creative thinking, however. By law, military roles for women were strictly defined and limited. Because the word "pilot" wasn't in the statutes, women couldn't serve in that capacity.

General Arnold and Jackie Cochran devised a compromise. The WASP would work for the army but not as members of the army. This meant the WASP pilots could leave service, or be "fired" without repercussions or justification. It also meant military benefits, including insurance, veterans' medical care, and the G.I. Bill that sent thousands of veterans to college, were denied them.

Jackie Cochran accepted this "work-without-benefits" situation. Her only alternative was to end the program altogether.

Flying, whether ferrying or in noncombat roles, was dangerous. The planes assigned to the WAFS and, later, WASP were often poorly maintained or just plain "old wrecks." Women pilots conducted test-flights to determine if repaired airplanes were flight worthy. The results were predictable.

Mabel Rawlinson died when an A-24 plane stalled, crashed, and caught fire. A broken cockpit latch trapped her. Fellow pilots heard her screams but couldn't reach her. Later, records showed the broken latch had been noted, but no repairs were done.

Cornelia Fort, a flight instructor in Pearl Harbor during the Japanese bombing in 1941, was the first of Nancy Love's pilots to die. Six male pilots and Cornelia ferried BT-13 planes from California to Dallas, Texas. One male pilot came so close to Cornelia's plane that the wingtip was damaged. Her plane spun out of control, and she died in the resulting crash.

The offending pilot was, at best, ignoring basic safety procedures. Accusations were made that he was actually attempting to intimidate Cornelia or "show off" to his fellow pilots. In the end no consequences resulted. The military didn't even ship Cornelia's coffin home to her family. The WAFS women collected money and accompanied her body home themselves.

By the war's end thirty-eight female pilots had died in training or flying. That said, safety records for women pilots were better than their male counterparts flying noncombat and ferrying missions.

As the war dragged on, ferrying operations were increasingly done by women. The WASP flew army antiaircraft training missions, pulling a long, canvas "sleeve" behind the plane. Gunners shot at the sleeve from the ground.

WASP flew bombers over desert areas so soldiers could learn to drop bombs. Maggie Gee, a Chinese-American and one of Nancy's "experts," trained men in instruments-only, "blind" flying.

When army pilots nicknamed one plane the "Flying Coffin" because of fires on takeoff, Nancy's pilots analyzed the problem and developed a special technique for takeoff and landing. With those techniques, the fire hazard was eliminated.

Nancy Love and Betty Gillies learned to fly the new B-17. This massive plane, sometimes dubbed the "Flying Fortress," was intimidating to many pilots.

By February 1944, with Jackie Cochran and Nancy Love still directing their operations separately, Congress drafted a bill to make the WASP part of the Army Air Corps.

However, in part because women pilots had freed their male counterparts for combat duty, the army closed its pilot training schools. Thousands of civilian flight instructors were scheduled for layoff. And, those men would lose their draft deferments. The women, somehow, were blamed. A campaign was launched to close the WASP and give their jobs to men.

Generals Arnold and Tunner fought for the women pilots. Reports were issued showing the women had done exceptional work, even in the face of discrimination and second-class treatment.

However, on June 21, 1944, Congress voted against making WASP part of the army. General Arnold wrote to every WASP, "When we needed you, you came through and have served most commendably under very difficult circumstances." However, the letter closed with the words, "the time has come when your volunteered services are no longer needed."

The women were crushed. Nancy Love had one hundred women trained as fighter pilots, with thousands of hours of air experience. She tried to find a way for her pilots to continue. Some base commanders petitioned the army, saying the women pilots were desperately needed. In the end, the army refused them all. One California base had fifty-one aircraft on the runway, with no pilots to fly them.

Nancy's pilots and the other WASP returned home. For some, adjustment was painful. Some returned to college. Others returned to marriage. Nancy and Bob Love kept flying and started a family. But none found commercial piloting work.

In twenty-six months Nancy Love had flown twenty-eight different kinds of airplanes and logged nearly one thousand hours in the air. After the war, Nancy Love received the Army's Air Medal.

For thirty years WAFS and WASP records were sealed. Three decades later, on September 10, 1976, the U.S. Senate voted to make members of the WASP official World War II veterans. During the yearlong battle it took for the U.S. House of Representatives to agree, Nancy Love died. On November 23, 1977, President Jimmy Carter signed the bill granting veteran status to Nancy Love's pilots and their WASP sisters.

BIBLIOGRAPHY

Magdelaine LaFramboise

Kinzie, Juliette (Mrs. John). *Wau-Bon, The Early Day of The Northwest.* Chicago: D.B. Cooke & Co., 1857.

Métis Women in the Fur Trade at Mackinac. www.rootsweb.com/.

Widder, Keith R. *Historic Women of Michigan,* chapter 1. Lansing, Mich.: Michigan Women's Studies Association, 1987.

Sojourner Truth

Bernard, Jacqueline. *Journey Toward Freedom: The Story of Sojourner Truth.* New York: Norton, 1967.

Douglass, Frederick. *The Life and Time of Frederick Douglass.* Hartford, Conn.: Park Publishers, 1881. Mineola, N.Y.: Dover Publications, 2003.

McLoon, Margo. *Sojourner Truth: A Photo Illustrated Biography.* Mankato, Minn.: Bridgestone Press, 1997.

Painter, Nell Irvin. *Sojourner Truth: A Life, a Symbol.* New York: W.W. Norton, 1996.

Robinson, Marius. *The Salem Anti-Slavery Bugle,* June 21, 1851.

Truth, Sojourner, and Olive Gilbert. *The Narrative of Sojourner Truth.* Boston: For the Author, 1875. Oxford, England: Oxford University Press, 1994.

Laura Smith Haviland

Burns, Virginia Law. *Bold Women*. Missoula, Mont.: Mountain Press, 2005.

Fields, Harriet. "Laura Haviland: Forceful, Fluent Humanitarian." *Daily Telegram,* June 26, 1975.

Haviland, Laura Smith. *A Woman's Life Work, Labors and Experiences of Laura S. Haviland*. Cincinnati, Ohio: Walden and Stowe, 1881.

Troester, Rosalie Riegle, editor. *Historic Women of Michigan*. Lansing, Mich.: Michigan Women's Studies Association, 1987.

Julia Wheelock Freeman

Abatt, Corinne. "Civil War buff finds heroine through diary." *Detroit Free Press,* undated.

Herdegen, Lance. *The Men Stood Like Iron*. Indianapolis: Indiana University Press, 1997.

Sullivan, Roderick B. "Biography of Julia Susan Wheelock." Wheelock Genealogy Home Page, www.wheelockgenealogy.com.

Wheelock, Julia S. *The Boys in White: The Experience of a Hospital Agent In and Around Washington*. New York: Lange and Hillman, 1870.

Sarah Emma Edmonds

Balkam, Rochelle. Unpublished article. Michigan Women's History Center, East Lansing.

Dannett, Sylvia. *She Rode with the Generals: The True and Incredible Story of Sarah Emma Seelye, Alias Franklin Thompson*. New York: Thomas Nelson & Sons Publishers, 1960.

Edmonds, Sarah Emma. *Memoirs of a Soldier, Nurse, and Spy. A Woman's Adventures in the Union Army.* De Kalb, Ill.: Northern Illinois University Press,1999.

Lammers, Pat, and Amy Boyce. "A Female in the Ranks: Alias Franklin Thompson." *Civil War Times,* January 1984, 24–30.

Seelye, S. Emma. Correspondence with Richard Halstead, Michigan Women's History Center Archival Collections.

Stuart, Damon. "Story of a Remarkable Life." Letter dated 1900, Michigan Women's History Center Archival Collections.

Anna Howard Shaw

Conway, Jill Ker. *Written by Herself.* New York: Random House-Vintage, 1992.

Croft, Margaret. "Anna Howard Shaw: Oak From the Forest." Mecosta County, Mich.: Mecosta County Women's Historical Council, undated.

Michigan League of Women Voters Bulletin. "Michigan to Memorialize Dr. Anna Shaw." January 1930.

Pohl, Keith I. "Unknown Heroine." *Michigan Christian Advocate,* February 1979.

Shaw, Anna Howard, D.D., M.D. *The Story of a Pioneer.* New York: Harper & Brothers Publishers, 1915.

Woodward, Helen Beal. "Anna H. Shaw—minister, doctor, champion of women." *Boston Globe,* February 23, 1974.

Rebecca Shelley

(Battle Creek, Michigan) *Enquirer.* "Globe-Circling Peace Pilgrim Dies at Age 97." 1984.

Reedy, Janet. "Synopsis of Life of Rebecca Shelley." Ann Arbor, Michigan: Bentley Historical Library, Rebecca Shelley Papers. Correspondence with Geraldine Blair, 1980.

Shelley, Rebecca. "Autobiographical Outline." Ann Arbor, Mich.: Bentley Historical Library, Rebecca Shelley Papers. Correspondence, August 1979.

———. *A Widow's Mite*. Battle Creek, Mich.: Peaceways, 1961.

———. *In Mourning for the War Dead*. Battle Creek, Mich.: Peaceways, 1971.

———. *Je m'accuse*. Battle Creek, Mich.: Peaceways, 1968.

Yagoda, Ben. "The True Story of Bernard McFadden." AmericanHeritage.com, *American Heritage Magazine,* 1981.

Ana Clemenc

Andrews, Clarence. "Big Annie and the 1913 Michigan Copper Strike." *Michigan History* LVII (1973) 53-68.

Murkowski, Carol. "Miner's wife carried banner for cause of 1913 strike." *Upbeat Magazine,* 1980.

Troester, Rosalie Riegle, ed. *Historic Women of Michigan*. Lansing, Mich.: Michigan Women's Studies Association, 1987.

Wendland, Michael. "The Calumet Tragedy." *American Heritage Magazine,* May 1986.

Marguerite Lofft de Angeli

Anderson, William. *Michigan's Marguerite deAngeli: The Story of Lapeer's Native Author-Illustrator.* Lapeer, Mich.: William Anderson, 1987.

de Angeli, Marguerite. *Butter at the Old Price*. New York: Doubleday & Company, 1971.

————. *Copper-Toed Boots.* Garden City, N.Y.: Doubleday & Company, 1938.

————. *The Door in the Wall.* Garden City, N.Y.: Doubleday & Company, 1949.

Marguerite de Angeli papers, Marguerite de Angeli Collection, Lapeer, Mich., District Library, undated.

Gwen Frostic

Barnes, Jim. "Still Going . . ." *Tri City Record Eagle,* December 1996.

Doud, Katherine. "Humor Dreams, Work and a Creative Life." *Kalamazoo Gazette,* April 1984.

Frostic, Bill. Interview. Benzonia, Mich., April 2006.

Gould, Rick. "The Art of Living and Working at 90." *Northern Expressions Magazine,* May 1996, 15.

James, Sheryl. *The Life and Wisdom of Gwen Frostic.* Chelsea, Mich.: Clock Tower Press, 1999.

Lorenz, Pam. Beulah, Mich. Frostic papers.

————. Interview. Benzonia, Mich., April 2006.

Northlands Gazette. "Gwen Frostic: It Just Comes Naturally." May 27, 1994.

Shellenbarger, Pat. "Well-Versed by Nature." *Grand Rapids Press,* undated.

Tessler, Sandra. "Gwen Frostic, Michigan's Most Unique Natural Resource. *Detroit News Magazine,* September 1986.

Weist, Janet. "Love of Art Keeps Her Going." *Flair Magazine,* July 28, 1996.

Rosa Parks

Brinkley, Douglas. *Rosa Parks.* New York: Viking Penguin, 2000.

Kohl, Herbert. *She Would Not Be Moved.* New York: The New Press, 2005.

Parks, Rosa, with Gregory J. Reed. *Quiet Strength.* Grand Rapids, Mich.: Zondervan Publishers, 1994.

Parks, Rosa, with Jim Haskins. *My Story.* New York: Puffin Books, 1992.

Summer, L.S. *Rosa Parks, Journey to Freedom Series.* Chanhassen, Minn.: The Child's World Inc., 2000.

Nancy Harkness Love

Douglas, Deborah G. "Wasps of War." *Aviation History Magazine,* undated reprint.

Haynesworth, Leslie, and David Toomey. *Amelia Earhart's Daughters.* New York: William Morrow & Co., 1998.

Keil, Sally VanWagenen. *Those Wonderful Women in Their Flying Machines.* New York: Warson, Wade Publishers, Inc., 1979.

"Nancy Harkness Love, Military Strategist." Dayton, Ohio: National Aviation Hall of Fame Web site, www.nationalaviation.blade6 .donet.com/.

Nathan, Amy. *Yankee Doodle Gals.* Washington, D.C.: National Geographic Society Publishers, 2001.

Rickman, Sarah Byrn. The Originals: The Women's Auxiliary Ferrying Squadron, World War II. www.disc-us.com. Disc-Us books, 2001.

ABOUT THE AUTHOR

Julia Pferdehirt is an author, storyteller, and history buff living in Madison, Wisconsin.

As a child growing up in Michigan she visited Gwen Frostic's studio. She will never forget long drives with her beloved grandmother and storyteller-grandfather through Michigan's beautiful countryside. He'd say, "Hey sis, let's go." And, many hours later they'd pull up in front of some tiny shop on the shores of Lake Michigan to buy smoked fish or blueberries or a bushel of apples.

In addition to this book, Pferdehirt's recent books include biographies *Independence Day: The Story of Caroline Quarles* and *The Blue Jenkins Story,* both with the Wisconsin Historical Society Press.

Award-Winning TwoDot Titles

The Women Writing the West Willa Literary Awards recognize outstanding literature featuring women's stories set in the West.

2006 WINNER— MEMOIR/ESSAY

The Lady Rode Bucking
Horses: The Story of
Fannie Sperry Steele,
Woman of the West
Dee Marvine

2006 FINALIST

Pioneer Doctor: The
Story of a Woman's Work
Mari Graña

2006 FINALIST

More Than Petticoats:
Remarkable
Nevada Women
Jan Cleere

2003 FINALIST

Strength of Stone:
The Pioneer Journal of
Electa Bryan Plumer,
1862–1864
A Novel by Diane Elliott

Available wherever books are sold

Orders can be placed on the Web at www.GlobePequot.com,
by phone at 1-800-243-0495, or by fax at 1-800-820-2329

TwoDot® is an imprint of The Globe Pequot Press